I0528230

Samson in the Valley of Sorek

A Reflective look at Becoming Spiritually Desensitized

Alvin Frank, M. Div.

Foreword by: Aaron A. M. Ross, Ph. D

Unless otherwise indicated, scripture references are taken from the Holy Bible, NEW INTERNATIONAL VERSION®, NIV® Copyright © 1973, 1978, 1984, 2011 by Biblica, Inc.® Used by permission. All rights reserved worldwide.

Scripture references marked (MSG) are taken from The Message. Copyright © by Eugene H. Peterson 1993, 1994, 1995, 1996, 2000, 2001, 2002. Used by permission of NavPress Publishing Group.

Scripture references marked (NASB) are taken from the New American Standard Bible®, Copyright © 1960, 1962, 1963, 1968, 1971, 1972, 1973, 1975, 1977, 1995 by The Lockman Foundation. Used by permission.

Scripture quotations marked (ESV) are taken from The Holy Bible, English Standard Version® (ESV®), copyright © 2001 by Crossway, a publishing ministry of Good News Publishers. Used by permission. All rights reserved.

Scripture quotations marked (NLT) are taken from the Holy Bible, New Living Translation, copyright ©1996, 2004, 2007 by Tyndale House Foundation. Used by permission of Tyndale House Publishers, Inc., Carol Stream, Illinois 60188. All rights reserved.

Scripture quotations marked (NKJV) are taken from the New King James Version®. Copyright © 1982 by Thomas Nelson, Inc. Used by permission. All rights reserved.

Scripture quotations marked (CSB) are taken from the Christian Standard Bible. Copyright © 2017 by Holman Bible Publishers. Used by permission. Christian Standard Bible®, and CSB® are federally registered trademarks of Holman Bible Publishers, all rights reserved.

Scripture quotations marked (KJV) are taken from the Holy Bible, King James Version, which is in the public domain.

Samson in the Valley of Sorek:
A Reflective Look at Becoming Spiritually Desensitized

Foreword by Aaron A.M. Ross

"In ministry, private purity is the source of public power",[1] writes Rick Warren. These words ring true not only for those in vocational ministry, but also those who minister in their homes, the marketplace, the academy, their communities, or anywhere else for that matter.[2]

Still, public purity is also important. Many of us are familiar with the question "who are you when nobody else is watching?" But the adverse, "who are you when *everybody* else is watching?" is as profound. Indeed, as social media likes, subscribes, and follows have become the opium of the masses, and where shock value provides click bait, the temptation has become not simply to stray in secret, but also to do so in full view. In an era of unprecedented moral relativism, the reminder to lead with spiritual integrity is more needed than ever.

---

[1] https://x.com/RickWarren/status/13199824941752321
[2] https://bible.alpha.org/en/classic/17/index.html

I have known Alvin Frank for fifteen years, throughout which I have always respected him as a leader of utmost integrity. Alvin is my friend, but I have often thought of Alvin even more as a pastor to pastors. Spiritual desensitization is real. One might even think of it as one of pastoral ministry's riskiest workplace hazards. Samson's life provides those ready to listen and learn with a cautionary tale. And in this book, Alvin, more than simply offering advice, pours out wisdom for those prepared to receive it.

As leaders in ministry, we must be ever mindful of the weight our words and actions carry. What we say and do, even in passing or jest, can ripple outward, impacting not just our reputation but the hearts and minds of those we serve.

It can feel easy to let down our guard in spiritually desensitized ways, especially when we feel comfortable in our circles. But comfort can be deceptive. Just as boundaries exist to safeguard our integrity, we must establish clear moral guardrails to ensure we do not lose sight of God's holiness.

Our spiritual integrity is not merely about staying out of trouble; it is about remaining faithful in all we say and do, even when it is inconvenient, unpopular, or difficult. This is how spiritual leaders set the tone for those they lead. Remaining spiritually sensitive is not just about scruples—it is a profound responsibility that requires us to take ourselves and our calling seriously.[3]

Alvin Frank's work, *Samson in The Valley of Sorek*, is more than just a reflection on Samson's story; it is a vital reminder for every leader about the dangers of spiritual desensitization. Alvin calls us to remain vigilant, to be leaders who, in a world of shifting moral standards, hold fast to spiritual integrity both in private and in public.

Alvin's insights are a gift to those willing to listen, and they offer a roadmap for leaders seeking to avoid the pitfalls that ensnared Samson. Alvin's wisdom is not theoretical—he lives what he teaches. And through this book, he extends a lifeline of guidance for those of us called to lead, reminding us that true and lasting influence in ministry comes from the overflow of hearts that remain dedicated to God.

Aaron A.M. Ross holds a PhD in Theology, Concentration in the History of Christianity, from the University of St. Michael's College in the University of Toronto (Wycliffe College). He is a settler Canadian historian of Christianity, an ordained minister with the Pentecostal Assemblies of Canada, Lead Pastor of Richmond

---

[3] Kent Ingle, *9 Disciplines of Enduring Leadership: Developing the Potential of Your Divine Design,* 2nd edition, (Greenbrier, TN: Self-published, Kent Ingle, 2023), 60-3.

Pentecostal Church, author of The Holy Spirit and the Eagle Feather: The Struggle for Indigenous Pentecostalism in Canada *(McGill-Queen's University Press, 2023) and instructor in the History of Christianity at Summit Pacific College. Aaron, his wife Annabel, and their two daughters live in Metro Vancouver, where they enjoy all that beautiful British Columbia has to offer.*

Acknowledgment

I dedicate this book to my loving wife Glenda, whose support, understanding and encouragement have enabled me to spend many hours in the preparation of this manuscript. For this, I am eternally grateful to her.

Thank you

Thanks to my former Pastor, Rev. Earl McNutt who spent nineteen years as Lead Pastor at the Stone Church in Toronto. He was instrumental in getting me started, at a very early age, in teaching the Adult Bible Class both on Sundays, and during the Mid-week Study. A true leader and a man of great integrity. I have just learned about his passing today, as I write this. He was ninety-five years of age. The Lord Jesus welcomes you home!

Thank you to Rev. Donald Noble (deceased) and his wife Carol-Anne who spent twenty years altogether, first as Associate Pastor and then as Lead Pastor at the Stone Church in Toronto. Don was instrumental in me joining the Pastoral Staff at the Stone Church, when I was through with my engineering career. He was a loving and dedicated husband, father, and friend, whose example as an incarnational leader and preacher of the word of God was worthy of emulation. He has left us way too soon, the victim of a rare form of cancer.

Thank you to Rev. Godfrey Adderley (wife Tania) the current Lead Pastor at the Stone Church in Toronto. He is a passionate preacher of the word of God – whose mission is fulfilling the Great Commission of Jesus Christ – Discipling others as we go. I am happy to be a member of his Discipleship Small Group for leaders. Over the past four years, his leadership skills and personal transparency, have enabled the group to stay accountable to one another.

Thanks to my Discipleship Small Group which I lead, and which keeps me accountable week by week as we study how to 'Abide in Jesus' as well as 'Growing in Godly Character.' Thanks to Jermaine, Claudia, Yomi, Tula, Gboyega, Grace, Tonika and Alice for your insights and faithfulness.

Thanks to Rev. Dr. Aaron M Ross, Ph. D., who has written the 'Foreword' for this book. I have known Aaron now for about fifteen years. Our paths crossed during our studies at Seminary. He is a dedicated follower of Jesus Christ, a great scholar, a committed husband and father, and someone I am delighted to call my friend.

And last but not least:

Thanks to my Tuesday Morning Prayer Group that faithfully gets together online for prayer for the needs of our country, our province, our city, our church and for the needs of our families. Thank you, Daniel, Alice, Rosalva, John, Kasahun, Colleen and

Marian. Thank you for your faithfulness. May the Lord continue to bless you.

Contents

Introduction

The setting would have been perfect. All his teammates and his former classmates were there. The church was packed with friends and family members. It would have been perfect, except they had all come to say their final goodbyes to Johnny – a member of the College and Careers Group.

Johnny, not his real name, of course, had grown up in the church. He was an 'A' student, a great athlete, a committed Christian, someone that the young people looked up to, and who had gained the admiration of the older folks.

He had received a scholarship and had moved away from home to pursue his dream studies at the University. He was in his final year when tragedy struck.

His former Pastor, Vincent (not his real name), who took the funeral service, said that at the University, Johnny got in with the wrong crowd. The pressure to conform was more than he could handle. And so little by little, Johnny drifted away - experimenting with alcohol and other hard drugs and becoming sexually promiscuous. Finally, he contracted some kind of sexually transmitted disease, from which he died of complications. He was 23 years of age.

Out in the lobby following the service, some of the ladies

were trying to come to grips with what had happened. "It is so hard to understand," one of them said. "How could this have happened to someone like Johnny?"

Another lady said, "They never really said exactly what he died from."

One lady who had been his Sunday school teacher said, "The Samson Syndrome." The Samson Syndrome, they asked?

She was no doubt referring to Samson, the 'strong man' of the Bible who had become a Judge and served for 20 years. He was anointed by God to deliver His people from the tyranny of the Philistines. They had invaded their land and had held them captive for many years.

Yes, like Samson, this young man took a walk on the wild side and couldn't get back. He just drifted away... He had found himself in an environment that was foreign to his own. Yet, knowing the dangers, he became comfortable and was lulled into a false sense of euphoria, which was so intoxicating that he was unable to discern the depth to which he had sunk.

Deep-water divers are a fearless bunch. Equipped with their SCUBA (self-contained underwater breathing apparatus), they can go to tremendous depths where it is peaceful and calm. But they will tell you that when they are under water at those extreme depths, there are several things of which they have to be aware. The first one is that they could lose track of time and run out of oxygen. Another would be the condition known as the bends - a condition arising from dissolved gases forming bubbles inside the body as the diver decompresses coming to the surface. But divers will tell you the thing they fear the most is a condition called nitrogen narcosis. This condition produces symptoms similar to drunkenness or the same effect of inhaling laughing gas.

Further increases in the partial pressure of nitrogen in the blood from descending deeper can lead to impairments in manual dexterity and further mental decline, including thought fixation, hallucinations, and finally, stupor and coma. Death can result from unconsciousness associated with severe narcosis or from severely impaired judgment, leading to an accident of some form during the dive. The symptoms seen in nitrogen narcosis begin first with effects of the higher function, such as judgment, reasoning, short-term memory, and concentration. The diver may also experience a euphoric or stimulating feeling initially, similar to mild alcohol intoxication.

There is a strange irony here. The diver feels very much at home in an environment that is totally foreign to his own and one which can prove fatal at a moment's notice. He basks almost playfully as a dolphin frolicking in the deep. But in this state of euphoria, as he enjoys the ride of these strange undercurrents, they can eventually take him to his death.

As a follower of Jesus, we, too are living in a foreign environment. The Scriptures tell us that we are 'strangers and pilgrims' in this world. And if we are not careful, we too can be lulled into a state of euphoria, where this hostile environment begins to dictate the standards by which we ought to live. Therefore, we have to pay careful attention so that our fascination with the lure of titillating experiences does not become a threat to our spiritual well-being and our kingdom values.

This book, "Samson in the Valley of Sorek" is written primarily for young adults who are in the process of making decisions about how they will live sexually, decisions about choosing a career, decisions about choosing a mate, decisions about where they will live and decisions about living a healthy spiritual life with Jesus Christ as Lord. It is written with the hope that you will learn from the miss-steps of such characters like Samson and others, who had been anointed by God to be a deliverer but who presumed on the grace and mercy of God and drifted away.

In addition, this book is written for pastors, caregivers, and leaders of any kind who, by virtue of their calling, usually find themselves in vulnerable situations. "Above all else, guard your heart, for it is the wellspring of life."

Metaphorically speaking, the Valley of Sorek is that beckoning gate that leads to the house of the enemy. It is that rope called pleasure that is tied to our waist, pulling us back to the things we do not want to do. The Valley of Sorek is that place where good and evil meet and the good is corrupted by evil. It is that place that looks good on the outside but it is a place of bitter and constant regrets. Sorek is a place of separation. It is a place where God's presence will never go with us - a place where God gave instructions never to go. The Valley of Sorek is that cleverly concealed sin we are committing, thinking, and hoping nobody will see us. Sorek is that place we visit in the dark, foolishly thinking God does not see us.

No, don't allow the deceitful attractiveness of sin that temporarily blinds the child of God and wraps its tentacles around your heart to cause you to become spiritually desensitized. But rather, you should live in close connection to Jesus Christ and allow His grace to keep on transforming you, moment by moment. Because He is the "True Vine," and we are the branches.

Additionally, it is written to older folks who have been on the journey of following Jesus for a long time but have become so familiar with the grace of God that they are beginning to take for granted what Jesus went to the cross to purchase for their salvation. Don't ever become careless with that which has been provided for you at such a great price, becoming so puffed up and self-reliant that you presume on the grace of Jesus Christ our Lord.

In the Epistle to the Hebrews, the writer gives this stern warning;

A Call to Faithfulness

We must pay more careful attention, therefore, to what we have heard so that we do not drift away. For if the message spoken by angels was binding, and every violation and disobedience received its just punishment, how shall we escape if we ignore such a great salvation? This salvation, which was first announced by the Lord, was confirmed to us by those who heard him. God also testified to it by signs, wonders and various miracles, and gifts of the Holy Spirit distributed according to his will (Hebrews 2:1-4).

A Bit of My Story

One of my earliest recollections as a child is of the morning when I was crawling around on the floor of our living room when one of my uncles passed by with a tiny white coffin on his shoulder. It contained my sibling, who had died at birth. I don't know how old I was at the time, probably a toddler. I didn't know exactly what was happening then, but I remember feeling that life was full of sadness. Including that deceased baby, there were nine children in the family. I was the fifth born, so I'm the quintessential middle child.

I was born in Trinidad and Tobago, on the smaller of the two islands, but moved to Trinidad to attend school when I was seventeen years old. I remember it clearly because it was a week following the death of my father, who passed away at the early age of fifty-nine. I had made all my plans to travel and was unable to change them. Suffice it to say, it was a very sad and lonely time of my life.

But two years later, on one of my summer vacations back in Tobago, something happened that changed my life for all eternity. One evening, as I was hurrying along the street to catch up with some former school friends, a young man stopped me in my tracks and introduced me to Jesus Christ. That evening, on the side of the street, I bowed my head and invited the Lord Jesus Christ into my heart. It was the most important and happiest decision I have ever made.

After graduation, I worked for a few years, after which I immigrated to Toronto, Canada. I started attending The Stone Church, where I have attended to this day. I studied Engineering Technology at Ryerson University (now TMU), and most of my working career was spent in engineering at Ontario's largest power generation company.

When I had the opportunity to retire early, I was invited to join the pastoral staff at my church. This opened the door for me to attend Tyndale Seminary, where I pursued Biblical and Pastoral Studies, graduating with a Master of Divinity degree in 2010. I held the position on staff as Discipleship & Care Pastor for seventeen years until my "retirement" in 2022.

I am passionate about the care of people and thank the Lord always that He has given me the desire to encourage His children. I trust that this book will cause you to take note of your own walk with the Lord and that by abiding in Him, you will be able to overcome the challenges and temptations that are so evident around us.

This book: "Samson the Valley of Sorek" - A Reflective Look at Becoming Spiritually Desensitized, is my second published work as an author. My first book is titled: "In Every Season" – 101 Devotionals for the Journey.

I am married to my wife, Glenda, and we have two daughters, Karen and Cathy.

Chapter 1
The Cycle of Sin, Judgment & Deliverance

The Book Judges chapter 13 begins this way:

Again, the Israelites did evil in the eyes of the LORD, so the LORD delivered them into the hands of the Philistines for forty years (Judges 13:1).

This verse of Scripture is reminding its readers that there is a repetitive cycle of evil that is taking place in the Israelite nation. Time and time again, Israel falls into sin and rebels against God; then God disciplines them – usually by sending another nation to carry out his bidding. Then Israel cries out to God, and God extends mercy to them and appoints a Judge to deliver them. After they have been delivered, there will be a period of peace. But that peace is never a lasting one. Because on and on they go, returning to their sinful and evil ways. Judges chapter 2 gives us a little synopsis of the kind of cycle that takes place.

> Then the LORD raised up judges, who saved them out of the hands of these raiders. Yet they would not listen to their judges but prostituted themselves to other gods and worshiped them. They quickly turned from the ways of their ancestors, who had been obedient to the LORD's commands. Whenever

the LORD raised up a judge for them, he was with the judge and saved them out of the hands of their enemies as long as the judge lived, for the LORD relented because of their groaning under those who oppressed and afflicted them. But when the judge died, the people returned to ways even more corrupt than those of their ancestors, following other gods and serving and worshiping them. They refused to give up their evil practices and stubborn ways (Judges 2:16-19).

The accounts in the book of Judges are sometimes very graphic. You might even say, "I can't believe this is in the Bible." But you see, the Bible is not just some sanitized book that you read to make you feel good. It portrays the human condition, which is as old as the world in which we live. And so, when we read the Book of Judges, what we see is really a reflection of our own culture and the darkness of the un-repentant heart. The stories and truths within the Book are not just archaic tales with no relevance for us today. Instead, the book of Judges cracks a window into the depths of the human condition.

Judges 21:25 could be called the "Big Idea" of the Book. It says:

Samson in the Valley of Sorek

"In those days Israel had no king; all the people did whatever seemed right in their own eyes" (Judges 21:25 NLT)

And so, even though we are living in the twenty first century, this statement is a very relevant one in our day. Because we cannot turn on the news without hearing case after case of violence, deception, and scams, to name a few, which are being perpetrated on unsuspecting folks, if we were to take this kind of lawlessness from a personal level to a national level, we will see that many today do not know or have abandoned the 'King of Kings' - who wants to be Lord of their lives - in order that they could do exactly what pleases them.

But like the Israelites in the days of the Judges, we have become spiritually desensitized. How did we become careless with the things of God, so much so that we are no longer alarmed by the things we see happening around us? As I set out to write this book, the word "desensitized" has been replaying in my mind frequently. I couldn't shake this feeling that God was speaking to me, so I began to study its deep meaning. Desensitization means to cause someone to be less affected by something. It also means to be made emotionally insensitive or calloused. As I gave this some thought, what I believed God was speaking to me became clear, and the word began to convict my heart.

Alvin Frank, M. Div.

In a world where the media and entertainment industries run rampant with fornication, explicit language, raging violence, nudity, drugs, adultery, and homosexuality, it's a challenge to keep oneself from seeing these things on a regular basis. But when I started meditating on what God requires of us through his word, so many questions began to arise from within me. Just how much can we control what we see? How many times do we willingly expose our spirits to things that the Lord detests? And how has being desensitized had a negative impact on our walk with Christ?

The process of desensitization works much like the process of erosion. When a rock is continually exposed to rough waters, little by little, the water carries away minute pieces of it until it eventually becomes worn down into a tiny pebble. Every time that we expose ourselves to the deceitfulness of sin, we give up a piece of our spirit's awareness of God's heart. We become less and less reactive to sin until, eventually, we are caught up in a lifestyle where we are no longer able to discern what is evil in the sight of God.

In John 14:16-17 Jesus says, *"And I will ask the Father, and he will give you another advocate to help you and be with you forever— the Spirit of truth. The world cannot accept him because it neither sees him nor knows him. But you know him, for he lives with you and will be in you."*

The part of this Scripture that stands out to me is this: "the world cannot accept the Spirit." Because of this exact principle, wherever the spirit of the world abides, the Spirit of God will not abide. The more of the world we allow in our lives, the more we are shutting out the Spirit of God.

The Holy Spirit is so crucial to the believer because He is the one that convicts us and keeps us on track with God's plan. Without the Holy Spirit, we are numb to sin, completely desensitized to it. Hebrews 3:12-13 says, *"See to it, brothers and sisters, that none of you has a sinful, unbelieving heart that turns away from the living God. But encourage one another daily, as long as it is called "Today," so that none of you may be hardened by sin's deceitfulness."* This passage is all about staying alert, aware, and conscious at all times so that we do not allow our consciences to be seared by exposure to sin.

The question still remains: "Is it possible to become re-sensitized? Is there a way to change our hearts and sinful behaviors to hate what God hates and love what God loves once we have been desensitized? The answer is a resounding yes! But how does one break the cycle of sin, consequence, and forgiveness and not have it repeated with such regularity? It was in this atmosphere of sin and judgment that God raised up the Judges, and more specifically, Samson.

Alvin Frank, M. Div.

Enters Samson

There were many Heroes and heroines who arose as Judges, that seemed to have the potential to save Israel. But in the end, each proved to be a broken savior that couldn't deliver. It was into this atmosphere of oppression, decay and human lawlessness that God sent forth another deliverer. His name was Samson. Samson came into the world out of a crisis of sorts. Like many of the great biblical characters God called and used, Samson's mother was barren. Barrenness is a kind of harbinger proclaiming the truth that only through the intervention of God, through His amazing provision, is true deliverance possible. Samson's mother, who is nameless in the Bible, joins other famous mothers who need God's intervention in order to conceive a child.

There are several stories of barren women in the Bible. Three of the four matriarchs, Sarah, Isaac's mother (Genesis 11:30), Rebekah, Jacob's mother (Genesis 25:21); and Rachel, Joseph's mother (Genesis 30:24) were all barren women before God in his faithfulness enabled them to conceive. Hannah, the mother of the prophet Samuel (1 Samuel 1-2), was also barren. Then there is the anonymous wife of Manoah, mother of Samson (Judges 13). And, of course, we mustn't forget Elizabeth, mother of John the Baptist (Luke 1:7).

As we once again reflect on Judges 13, we find this account; Judges 13:2-3:

> A certain man of Zorah, named Manoah, from the clan of the Danites, had a wife who was childless, unable to give birth. The angel of the Lord appeared to her and said, "You are barren and childless, but you are going to become pregnant and give birth to a son" (Judges 13:2-3)

God had looked at her barrenness and decided that he was going to open her womb so that she could conceive a child. God was going to make Samson a Judge to deliver his people from the tyranny of the Philistines. But there were some conditions that had to be followed.

> "Now see to it that you drink no wine or other fermented drink and that you do not eat anything unclean. You will become pregnant and have a son whose head is never to be touched by a razor because the boy is to be a Nazirite, dedicated to God from the womb. He will take the lead in delivering Israel from the hands of the Philistines" (Judges 13:4-5).

One might ask, "Why were so many prominent women in the Bible barren? The "barren woman," as a literary paradigm in the

Bible, tells us about the relationship between God and God's chosen people. In the case of the patriarchal stories in Genesis, the matriarchs' barrenness emphasizes that it is God who acts sovereignly in the transition from one generation to the next and selects the true heir to the covenant. In the case of Samson, however, he was chosen to bring deliverance to God's people.

The Vow of the Nazarite

> The LORD said to Moses, "Speak to the Israelites and say to them: 'If a man or woman wants to make a special vow, a vow of dedication to the LORD as a Nazirite, they must abstain from wine and other fermented drink and must not drink vinegar made from wine or other fermented drink. They must not drink grape juice or eat grapes or raisins. As long as they remain under their Nazirite vow, they must not eat anything that comes from the grapevine, not even the seeds or skins. During the entire period of their Nazirite vow, no razor may be used on their head. They must be holy until the period of their dedication to the LORD is over; they must let their hair grow long. Throughout the period of their dedication to the LORD, the Nazirite must not go near a dead body. Even if their own father or mother or brother or sister dies, they must not make themselves

ceremonially unclean on account of them, because the symbol of their dedication to God is on their head. Throughout the period of their dedication, they are consecrated to the LORD." (Numbers 6:1-8)

The word Nazirite (can also be spelled Nazarite) is from the Hebrew term *nazir*, meaning "to consecrate," and is derived from the Hebrew root *nazar*, meaning "to separate". The man or woman who took the Nazirite vow took an oath to separate himself or herself from the world and even from close kinship affiliation to serve only the Lord, making the Nazirite totally "holy unto the Lord."

The vow of a Nazirite could be a special service performed for a certain length of time, or the vow could tie the Nazirite to a lifetime of service. According to the requirements of a Nazirite in Numbers 6:1-21, for the period of time in which the vow is in place, the Nazirite must:

1. Make a formal swearing of an oath of service to God (Numbers 6:2)

2. Abstain from drinking wine and fermented liquor, including vinegar derived from either wine or any fermented liquor, and abstain from eating grapes fresh or dried or eat anything that comes from the vine (Numbers 6:3-4).

3. Let his hair grow uncut for the length of the vow (Numbers 6:5)

4. For the entire period of the vow, he must not come in contact with a corpse. He is to remain ritually clean and cannot defile his ritual cleanliness, even in the event a parent or sibling dies (Numbers 6:7).

In the vow of the Nazirite, there is not only the concept of separation and consecration of an individual to God but also the concept of ministerial service. When a Nazirite completed a vow, he or she was to cut his or her hair and present the locks of hair, which represented the duration of the oath of service, at the Temple in Jerusalem, where it was to be burned on the sacrificial Altar with animal and grain sacrifices. The sacrificial requirements for a completed vow were an expensive undertaking, and often, wealthy Jews would sponsor a poor Nazirite who had completed a vow. The required offerings are described in Numbers 6:13-21.

Mostly, the vow was made for a limited time - usually 30 days. Samson, however, was to be a Nazirite all his life. It is interesting that there are only three people mentioned in Scripture who were Nazirites their entire life - Samson, Samuel, and John the Baptist. I say interesting because they were all born to women who were barren - Manoah's wife, Hannah, and Elizabeth. It just goes to show that God is a God who gives life to the dead and makes the barren fruitful. Isn't that awesome? In Isaiah 54:1, the prophet encourages the barren woman and tells her to rejoice.

"Sing, O childless woman, you who have never given birth! Break into a loud and joyful song, O Jerusalem, you who have never been in labor. For the desolate woman now has more children than the woman who lives with her husband," says the LORD (Isaiah 54:1 NLT).

The Birth of Samson

As Judges 13 continues, we see that Manoah had an encounter with the angel of the Lord. Manoah took a young goat, together with the grain offering, and sacrificed it on a rock to the LORD. And the LORD did an amazing thing while Manoah and his wife watched - the flame blazed up from the altar toward heaven, and then the angel of the LORD ascended in the flame. When Manoah and his wife saw this, they fell with their faces to the ground. They were both terrified at what they had seen, which made Manoah believe that they were doomed to die. But Manoah's wife said with great assurance,

"If the LORD had meant to kill us, he would not have accepted a burnt offering and grain offering from our hands, nor shown us all these things or now told us this." (Judges 13:23)

It was into this society where everyone did what was right in his or her eyes that Samson was born. Will his presence in his community break the cycle of sin and judgment? Or will he himself fall prey to the spirit of lawlessness? Will the anointing of the Lord that stirred his heart at a very early age be revered and cherished, or will it become so familiar that it is taken for granted? As we embark on this journey with this 'strong man', let us guard our own hearts so that we do not fall prey to the deceitful attractiveness of sin.

Chapter 2

When the Spirit of the Lord Stirs

Even though Samson had taken the Nazirite Vow, it was all external and the impact of it couldn't be realized until God anointed him with the Holy Spirit and blessed him. His wows would have been meaningless and totally dependent on his willpower unless God imbued him with power from on high. So, as the Lord blessed him, the Spirit of the Lord began to stir him.

I remember the night when I first wowed to serve the Lord for the rest of my life. I was inspired by what I had heard, and I felt like I could walk on water. In making the vow, I had purposed in my heart to keep it. But it wasn't long before I realized that in my own strength, regardless of my ardent desire, I wasn't going to be able to live up to my vow to follow Jesus. I needed more! I needed someone outside myself to help me to fulfill my desire to follow Jesus. So, one night, as a teenager in one of our services in a little church in Woodbrook, Port-of-Spain, Trinidad, God anointed me with His Holy Spirit and gave me an empowerment that was outside myself.

The two verses at the end of chapter 13 are all that we are told about Samson's birth, his childhood, and his becoming a man. It is all that we are told about his preparation to be a judge and deliverer in Israel before he was anointed by God to commence his ministry.

13

Alvin Frank, M. Div.

The woman gave birth to a boy and named him Samson. He grew and the LORD blessed him, and the Spirit of the LORD began to stir him while he was in Mahaneh Dan, between Zorah and Eshtaol (Judges 13:24-25).

When we come to Judges chapter 14, we meet Samson as a grown man seeking a wife and at the beginning of his work for God.

It is so often the case in biographies that so little is preserved concerning the early formative years of the person's life being recorded - those details which made the person who they were, formed their character and developed their gifts and talents. Those details of their early lives might have been very interesting, nevertheless, we are deprived of them. This is particularly true when we come to the stories of God's people.

In the case of 'John the Baptist,' we first encountered him when he was eight days old and his parents had brought him to the ceremony of circumcision and naming of the child. The gospel of Luke, chapter 1, tells us that his father, Zachariah, who had been rendered without speech at the beginning of Elizabeth's pregnancy on account of his unbelief, spoke up regarding the naming of the child. Zachariah said:

"His name is John." Immediately, his mouth was opened, and his tongue set free, and he began to speak, praising God. All the neighbors were filled with awe, and throughout the hill country of

Judea, people were talking about all these things. Everyone who heard this wondered about it, asking, "What then is this child going to be?" For the Lord's hand was with him (Luke 1:63-66).

As it was in the case of Samson, we did not encounter John the Baptist again until he began his ministry around the Jordan in the Judean Desert. We have not been told of his development during those early days. But the power and authority with which he spoke could have resulted only from the anointing of the Holy Spirit, as in the school of 'hard knocks' God was preparing him for ministry. Luke chapter 3 says;

During the high priesthood of Annas and Caiaphas, the word of God came to John, son of Zechariah, in the wilderness. He went into all the country around the Jordan, preaching a baptism of repentance for the forgiveness of sins (Luke 3: 2-3).

So those details of John's early life might have been very interesting, but we are deprived of them.

This is particularly true when we come to Jesus. Similarly, after his birth and the subsequent escape of his parents along with Jesus to Egypt, nothing was heard about him until he was about the age of twelve. He and his parents had gone up to Jerusalem at the time of his consecration. Thinking that he was with relatives, he was inadvertently left behind at the temple.

After three days, they found him in the temple courts, sitting among the teachers, listening to them and asking them questions. Everyone who heard him was amazed at his understanding and his answers. When his parents saw him, they were astonished. His mother said to him, "Son, why have you treated us like this? Your father and I have been anxiously searching for you." "Why were you searching for me?" he asked. "Didn't you know I had to be in my Father's house?" But they did not understand what he was saying to them (Luke 2:46-50).

During those formative years, although we are not told, we are confident that Jesus was being anointed by the Holy Spirit in preparation for his ministry. We will not see him again until he performed his first miracle at a wedding in Cana in Galilee by turning water into wine, when the host ran out of wine (John 2:1-11). It is evident, therefore, that without the anointing of the Holy Spirit, who stirs us and prepares us for ministry, good intentions and vows will amount to nothing. But after we have been anointed by the Spirit, we must keep that anointing alive by abiding in God. Because if we should ever take it for granted, we will become weak and powerless.

Samson in the Valley of Sorek

What is true here in Samson's case as well as in John the Baptist's and Jesus' is that what seems to be so little and unknown to us is in fact, much more than we realize. Their very absence is especially illuminating and instructive. We are told in these short accounts of the beginnings of Samson's life as well as John the Baptist and Jesus, where all blessing and success in the Christian life comes from. It comes from God, the giver of all good things.

We are told two things about Samson's early life, but how important and profound they are! We are told firstly that as Samson grew up, God blessed him. Then, secondly, we are told that the Spirit of the Lord began to stir him, giving him a foretaste of God's special power provided for him in his future work and that this foretaste enabled him to be a great man of God, with great power and strength in his work of deliverance.

"He grew, and the Lord blessed him". By this, we learn the greatness of God's gracious action in the life of Samson, which is the gracious action of God in the life of every believer. It tells us that Samson owed everything to God. God's blessing is the constant intervention and action in his life that enabled him to grow up strong both physically and spiritually. It meant, first of all, that God gave him Godly parents but also endowed those parents with spiritual life and gifts so that they were able to impart to their son the knowledge of God and what it meant to trust and live for God.

It was the gift of a godly home where Samson would grow up to know that God was real and was his sovereign Lord, where by example and practice, Samson would grow up to know God and worship him. Happy is the child who has this blessing of godly parents, where family prayers, grace at mealtime, and faith and submission to God permeate the whole of family life. This was part of the blessing of God upon Samson. We saw this gift of blessing in the way God chose Manoah and his wife to be his parents and instructed them on the task. The blessing given by God at this formative time in the life of Samson was in the means of grace by which Samson was able to profit - the grace of the true worship of God, which he was able to experience and in which he would actively engage.

Notice here that the secret of the spiritual life is not in any special talents and abilities we may have. These may make us into great people as the world sees it. We may become political leaders, or leaders in industry or in education, or be skilled in craft or art, but abilities bring no spiritual life or gifts. The secret of a spiritual life which we see in Samson, is the intervention of God, enhancing his natural gifts and abilities, and endowing him with special gifts. It is the grace of God regenerating the soul so that Samson has new life in him. And what he does for Samson, he does for us.

This blessing is more than the common grace of God that everyone enjoys, where God gives life, breath and everything else that we may enjoy in life. It was the special grace of God that saved and redeemed. This new life caused Samson to know where acceptance of God could be found. It was not with the clarity of the New Testament, but it was the same knowledge and faith. Just as we are accepted before God solely through the sacrifice of Jesus, Samson was given the blessing of God so that he knew where he could live in the favour of God.

This statement that God blessed Samson is so pregnant with meaning. It is not simply a general statement of God's goodwill towards him but a statement of God's electing grace claiming him for eternity. How much Samson and all God's redeemed have to thank God for! We are what we are because we stand in the grace of God solely by the sovereign and continual everlasting blessing of God. It is a blessing that will never let us go whatever we are like, as we shall see so markedly in the life of Samson.

This grace for Samson is described as the Spirit of the Lord stirring within him. We shall become familiar with this action of God as we progress in the life of Samson. What was its nature in the case of Samson? As we read Samson's story, we shall find that when God wanted him to work in deliverance, the Spirit of God came upon him and not only gave him supernatural power for the task ahead but also the indication of the will of God and what God had in mind for him to do.

God's blessing on Samson in these early days was that God began to teach him by experience concerning this equipment for his ministry. God gave him the experience of it so that he may be able to discern it when it came and not be in any doubt when the Spirit of the Lord was upon him. He was given the experience so that he could interpret and understand correctly when the Spirit of God was sent to him.

God is faithful, and he always equips his children with the task to which he calls them. He never calls us to work without giving the special necessary power by His Spirit to fulfill that work. We are told in Paul's first letter to the Corinthians chapter 12 that to each one, the manifestation of the Spirit is given for the common good. This is a special power for the ministry, which God has called each person to do. God does not send his people into the spiritual battle without the resources necessary to do his work.

There is a very important lesson here for all of us. Whatever our ministry, we must wait for the stirring of the Spirit before we act. In all the work of the church of God, we must be sure that we are moved by the Spirit of God and that true guidance of God has been given before we act. We must plead with God to make his will and way plain. We must be in godly fear that we never act outside the stirring of God. We must ask to be able to discern when this stirring is present. This is essential because it is only when God stirs his church to action or ministry he will accompany that ministry with blessing. Invariably, if we act without this stirring, evil consequences will usually follow.

As can be seen, Samson had a great start. A child appointed even before he was born by God to be a deliver of his people. He was blessed with great parents, and was anointed by the Lord and was filled with the Holy Spirit of God at a very early age. He had so much going for him! Would he abide in the Spirit or be overcome by his own carnal desires? Would he be a man of God to the very end, or would he presume upon the grace of God and trample underfoot, the blessing and favor God had extended to him?

Experience tells us that sometimes, blessed people become 'too big for their britches' – they mistake their prosperity for something that they have accomplished in their own strength and presume upon God's grace, taking it for granted, mistaking his kindness and his patience for a license to immoral living, which ultimately results in the downward spiral that leads to death. Sometimes, discovery is made in the time when we have been playing "Russian Roulette" with the Grace of God - trifling with His patience and trampling on his grace. But in the absence of this discovery and by taking actions that are inappropriate, we usually end with a great fall.

Chapter 3

The Downward Spiral that Leads to Death

In Judges chapter 14, Samson begins his descent, taking a ride on the wild side. With youthful passion and total disregard for God's known command, he sees the 'forbidden fruit', and it is pleasant to the eyes, so he decides that he must satisfy his carnal desires. This was his first misstep, going out of the will of God. Judges 14:1-2 tell us;

Samson went down to Timnah and saw there a young Philistine woman. When he returned, he said to his father and mother, "I have seen a Philistine woman in Timnah; now get her for me as my wife" (Judges 14:1-2).

Here, a grown-up Samson finally goes down to Timnah, the Philistine-controlled area. And what exactly does he do there, fight and begin the deliverance of Israel, maybe? Well, no, not exactly. He eyes up a Philistine woman whom he, oh sooo, wants! And so begins a sad tale where Samson goes down in more than just location. He goes down in morals, purity and separation unto God as a Nazirite.

Now, for anyone else except an Israelite, there would have been nothing wrong with that request. But one of God's prohibitions to the children of Israel was that they were not to inter-marry with people outside of the Israelite tribes.

This is what the Lord said to the children of Israel:

When the LORD your God brings you into the land you are entering to possess and drives out before you many nations—the Hittites, Girgashites,

Amorites, Canaanites, Perizzites, Hivites and Jebusites, seven nations larger and stronger than you— and when the LORD your God has delivered them over to you, and you have defeated them, then you must destroy them totally. Make no treaty with them, and show them no mercy. Do not intermarry with them. Do not give your daughters to their sons or take their daughters for your sons, for they will turn your children away from following me to serve other gods, and the LORD's anger will burn against you and will quickly destroy you (Deuteronomy 7:1-4)

Sometimes, young adults seeking a mate and have read this prohibition may ask the question, "Is God a racist?" the answer is a resounding no! God, in his sovereignty, knows that when two people of differing beliefs get together in a matrimonial bond, the possibility exists that one will turn the other away from following

God and toward the things of the world. In the case of the Israelites - to serve other gods. That's why we see, carried over into the New Testament, this same prohibition in 2 Corinthians 6:14;

Do not be yoked together with unbelievers. For what do righteousness and wickedness have in common? Or what fellowship can light have with darkness? (2 Corinthians 6:14)

Keenly aware of this prohibition, Samson's parents tried vigorously to dissuade him from taking a wife from among the Philistine nation.

His father and mother replied, "Isn't there an acceptable woman among your relatives or among all our people? Must you go to the uncircumcised Philistines to get a wife?" (Judges 14:3)

But Samson knew what he wanted and was quite persistent in conveying his intent to his parents. What his eyes had seen, and his heart desired made him totally 'blind' and 'deaf' to the protestations of his parents.

But Samson said to his father, "Get her for me. She's the right one for me." (His parents did not know that this was from the LORD, who was seeking an occasion to confront the Philistines; for at that time they were ruling over Israel.) (judges 14:3-4)

The writer of the Book of Judges added the phrase *(His parents did not know that this was from the LORD, who was seeking an occasion to confront the Philistines; for at that time they were ruling over Israel.)*

While the scripture does say that 'it was of the Lord' we should not ever think that this was God's desire for Samson. God's will is never in contradiction to His word, and the Bible clearly commanded Israel not to take women from the nations as their wives (Deuteronomy 7:3-4). At times, God will use our miss-steps for his own benefit and his own purposes. God will use this unholy alliance for His own good, but one cannot help but think of how God could have used Samson had his heart truly been toward the Lord. No compromising alliances were needed when God commissioned Othniel, Gideon or any of the other Judges, and one wasn't required here either!

The apostle James makes this perfectly clear for us to understand. James says; *When tempted, no one should say, "God is tempting me." For God cannot be tempted by evil, nor does he tempt anyone, but each person is tempted when they are dragged away by their own evil desire and enticed. Then, after desire has conceived, it gives birth to sin, and sin, when it is full-grown, gives birth to death* (James 1:13-15).

One cannot help but see a parallel here to the fictitious hero Superman. Just as Superman was vulnerable to 'kryptonite', so Samson had a chink in his armor through which his greatness was sapped. He was king of the hill when it came to physical prowess, but when it came to women and sexuality, he was a pawn of his own passions. Now, for many of us, our 'kryptonite' may not be Philistine women. We may be tempted by something else. But whatever it is, take extra care in that area and stay true to the scripture that says, *'put on the Lord Jesus, and make no provision for the flesh to fulfill its lusts, to gratify its desires'* (Romans 13:14). In response to this verse, each of us needs to ask: When, where, and with whom are we most tempted to accommodate our flesh and gratify its desires?

So Samson and his parents went down to Timnah, undoubtedly to ask for this young Philistine maiden's hand in marriage, and while on the road, Samson famously killed an attacking lion, and its carcass would later become home for a swarm of honey-producing bees.

Samson went down to Timnah together with his father and mother. As they approached the vineyards of Timnah, suddenly a young lion came roaring toward him. The Spirit of the LORD came powerfully upon him so that he tore the lion apart with his bare hands as he might have torn a young goat. But he told neither his father nor his mother what he had done. Then he went down and talked with the woman, and he liked her (Judges 14:5-7).

However, when Samson returned later to take his bride, he turned aside to look at the carcass of the lion, and amazingly, there was a swarm of bees that had made honey in the body of the lion. So he scraped the honey into his hands and went on, eating as he went. When he came to his father and mother, he gave some to them, and they ate it, but he did not tell them that he had scraped the honey out of the body of the lion.

Curiosity Leads to Compromise

Wow! What amazing strength Samson had! Out comes the lion, roaring away and ready for the kill. Yet it is no match for a Samson, supernaturally empowered by the Holy Spirit! This is the first time we are told of '*the Spirit of the Lord coming mightily upon him.*' Samson will encounter the Spirit of the Lord many times more, but what did this empowerment do for his character and confidence?

No sooner had Samson performed this great feat of strength, however, he was breaking his Nazirite vow by examining and touching the dead body of the lion! He seemed to have so little regard for the commands of the Lord. He *'turned aside to look at the carcass of the lion,'* the Bible says, and this curiosity with that which he wasn't allowed to do, led to compromise. Curiosity concerning sin has a habit of doing that!

On finding honey within the carcass of the lion, Samson took some home for his parents but made sure he didn't tell them where he got it from. It's not exactly surprising, as a guilty conscience often shuts our mouth from speaking the complete truth. The sweet honey may have given him temporary satisfaction, but was it really worth it, Samson? Like honey, sin can be temporarily satisfying. The Bible doesn't speak of the 'passing pleasure of sin' without reason (Hebrews 11:25). But it also speaks of the 'hardening' and 'deceitfulness' of sin (Hebrews 3:13). Thus, it promises much, but in the end only leaves emptiness. We must learn from Samson's error and don't let our curiosity lead to compromise.

The downward slide gains momentum...

Now, his father went down to see the woman. And there Samson held a feast, as was customary for young men. When the people saw him, they chose thirty men to be his companions (Judges 14:10-11).

So what started out as one Philistine companion now leads to thirty more! As Samson eats and drinks (and possibly breaks his Nazarite vow once again) at the feast to celebrate his soon-coming marriage, it probably doesn't even cross his mind that these same Philistines, his companions, are meant to be the ones from whom he is supposed to be delivering Israel! Strange way of deliverance indeed as Samson slowly starts to become more like those from whom he was meant to deliver Israel.

Through a strange set of circumstances regarding a riddle, which his Philistine companions were supposed to solve before the end of the seven-day feast, they were able to come up with the right answer just in the nick of time by pestering Samson's wife, who in turn pestered Samson for the answer until he relented, and gave her the answer. This so infuriated Samson that he went on a rampage.

Samson said to them, "If you had not plowed with my heifer, you would not have solved my riddle." Then the Spirit of the LORD came powerfully upon him. He went down to Ashkelon, struck down thirty of their men, stripped them of everything and gave their clothes to those who had explained the riddle. Burning with anger, he returned to his father's home. and Samson's wife was given to one of his companions who had attended him at the feast (Judges 14:18-20).

So this Philistine woman with whom he was so deeply in love slipped through his fingers due to the trickery of her people, and Samson embarked on a series of wildly violent campaigns against the Philistines (which also resulted in the horrible burning of the woman and her father — (Judges 15:6). As Samson took up residence in the cleft of the Rock of Etam, the Philistines retaliated by invading Judah. The men of Judah decided to hand Samson over to their enemies at Lehi, and Samson responded to that endeavor by picking up a donkey's jawbone and struck down a thousand Philistines with it (Judges 15:15). To commemorate this event, Samson named the place Ramath-Lehi.

Samson might have done well to ask himself why he was having this fight with the lion in the first place. Just maybe he should have taken it as a sign that going down after this Philistine woman was putting him in dodgy territory! The same could be possible for us. Not always, as Satan loves to attack those who are of the greatest use to the Lord... but clearly, this was a sign to Samson as a warning of things to come.

Chapter 4
Beware of the Philistines

Who were the Philistines?

The Bible references many ancient nations and peoples, with one of the most prominent ones being the Philistines. They were a tribe that inhabited the southern portion of the Land of Canaan, or the Promised Land to the Jewish people, that sits in modern-day Israel, but more specifically on and near the western coast. Originally from the Mediterranean, they made the Southern Levant their home for centuries until 604 BCE. They were often viewed as uncivilized or brutal, but their history shows that they were more complex than that.

The Philistines were one of the Israelite's greatest enemies in the Bible. During the famous Exodus from Egypt, the Israelites were forced to take a southern route to the Promised Land to avoid Philistine settlements. The Philistines were known for their advanced weaponry and formidable military and would be at odds with the Israelites and attempt to infringe on their land. The feud with the Israelites was because of land claims and because they were not what the Israelites considered civilized. They were considered uncircumcised pagan and ate pork, which was considered not kosher by the Jews.

They were also believed to be ethnically related to the ancient Egyptians. According to the book of Genesis, they were descendants of Ham, one of the three sons of Noah. One of Ham's sons was named Mizraim, which typically translates from Hebrew as "Egypt." Ironically, they attempted to attack Egypt and several other coastal civilizations before settling in Israel. As such, they were deemed the "Sea People" by other eastern Mediterranean civilizations.

In the Bible, the Philistines are remembered as an uncircumcised people with advanced technology and a formidable military (Judges 14:3; 1 Samuel 13:19–20; Exodus 13:17). The Philistines frequently encroached on Israelite territory, which led to some battles, including the famous clash between David, the Israelite, and Goliath, the Philistine (1 Samuel 17). They were condemned for being idol worshipers (1 Samuel 5:1–5) and soothsayers (Isaiah 2:6). In short, the Philistines are portrayed quite negatively in the Bible.

What marked the Philistines in the days of Abraham and Isaac was their striving to deprive God's servants of the water He had provided for them. Abraham had to reprove "*Abimelech because of a well of water, which Abimelech's servants had violently taken away*" (Genesis. 21:25), and when Isaac dwelt in Gerar, he found "all the wells which his father's servants had dug in the days of Abraham, his father, had been filled up with earth." (Genesis.

26:15). When Isaac "dug again the wells of water, the Philistines strove with him, so that he called the one Esek, which means "Quarrel," and the other Sitnah, which means "Opposition."

There are many mentions of the Philistines in the Book of Judges. By far, most of these are in connection with Samson. In Chapter 3, it says that the Philistines were left in the land by God, along with remnants of the Canaanites, to test Israel to know whether they would hearken unto the commandments of the Lord, which God commanded their fathers by the hand of Moses" (Judges 3:3-4). God did not destroy them as He had the nations of the land of Canaan, for if in the destruction of the nations of Canaan, we see the power of Satan broken, in the Philistines, we see the power of Satan still active, as God allowed them to test His people to see if they would remain faithful to his word.

God had marked the set time of forty years for this oppression and had prepared a deliverer who would "*begin to deliver Israel out of the hand of the Philistines*" (Judges 13:5). How very solemn it is to contemplate that God, in His sovereignty, has allowed His people, down through the centuries, to be oppressed by the nations of this world. Satan has taken the occasion of the failure of God's people to oppress them, and God has allowed him to do it so that His people might cry out to Him for deliverance.

David's Battle Against Them

As we have seen, God had prepared a deliverer who would *"begin to deliver Israel out of the hand of the Philistines"* (Judges 13:5). This tells us that Samson's mission from God wasn't to annihilate the Philistines but to begin the deliverance of God's people. Here we see some 50 years after Samson's defeat of the Philistines at their temple, killing about 3000 of them, the Philistines were still around in David's time. They had been defeated on many occasions, but they were still around.

Goliath stood and shouted to the ranks of Israel, "Why do you come out and line up for battle? Am I not a Philistine, and are you not the servants of Saul? Choose a man and have him come down to me. If he is able to fight and kill me, we will become your subjects; but if I overcome him and kill him, you will become our subjects and serve us" (1 Samuel 17:8-9).

According to Goliath, there was no need for a great deal of bloodshed. Why not let this conflict be settled by a fight between two champions: Goliath and whoever Israel designates to be their champion? We all know that Saul should have been Israel's champion. He was the king of Israel, who was expected to lead the army into battle. Furthermore, he was the man who stood head and shoulders above any other Israelite. But Saul was afraid and had no inclination to rise to the challenge put forth by Goliath, and his fear was contagious; all of the Israelite soldiers were afraid of Goliath and fled from him.

So it had been some years now since Samson's encounter with the Philistines. Their numbers would have grown significantly. The Philistines may well have outnumbered the Israelites, as well as outclassed them in terms of weaponry. It does not appear that the Israelites had iron weapons (except for Saul and Jonathan), nor did they have chariots, as did the Philistines. This would have caused the Israelites to have been very reluctant to engage the Philistines in battle in the valley, on level ground.

The Israelites would have wanted to wage war in the hills, where chariots would be of no use and where a giant laden down with armor and weapons would find it difficult to navigate. (Can you envision a nine-foot-tall soldier climbing uphill, over rocks and through the trees?) Besides, these Judean hills would have been familiar territory to the Israelite soldiers, who could wage a kind of gorilla warfare from there. But not to the Philistines. They were "flatlanders" who lived on the coastal plains. There, chariots would have been an awesome part of their weaponry. But they would not have been nearly as confident fighting in the hill country without the use of their chariots.

Alvin Frank, M. Div.

David on the Scene

As he was talking with them, Goliath, the Philistine champion from Gath, stepped out from his lines and shouted his usual defiance, and David heard it. Whenever the Israelites saw the man, they all fled from him in great fear (1 Samuel 17:23-24).

David asked the men standing near him, "What will be done for the man who kills this Philistine and removes this disgrace from Israel? Who is this uncircumcised Philistine that he should defy the armies of the living God?" (1 Samuel 17:26)

Yes, in David's time, the uncircumcised Philistines were still around. Apparently, they had grown in number since the days of Samson, and their weaponry was superior. But they were in for a rude awakening.

> He said to David, "Am I a dog that you come at me with sticks?" And the Philistine cursed David by his gods. "Come here," he said, "and I'll give your flesh to the birds and the wild animals!" David said to the Philistine, "You come against me with sword and spear and javelin, but I come against you in the name of the LORD Almighty, the God of the armies of Israel, whom you have defied (1 Samuel 17:43-45).

So when Goliath was asking the Israelites to send him a champion who would fight against him, he did not count on the Lord Almighty. Through the power of God, David was able to defeat Goliath, and subsequently, the Philistines were compelled into exile in Babylonia, where, over time, they lost their unique ethnic identity. By the late fifth century BC, they vanished from both historical and archaeological records as a distinct group. And so it is in our day, our weapon against the 'Philistines' is the Lord Almighty.

Today's Philistines

From the Scriptures we have considered, it must be evident that the Philistines represent *the* power of the enemy that the Lord allows for the discipline and chastening of His people when they transgress against Him. So it is natural for us to see the 'Philistines' in our modern day to be a metaphor for the power of the enemy that is constantly waging war against the believer today. So we must be on guard, first of all, so that we do not make any unholy alliances with them, and secondly, that we put on the full armor of God so that we can take our stand against the devil's schemes.

In Judges chapter 3, we see God leaving the Philistines in the land to discipline and test the people to see if they would be obedient to his word. If we look at that in context, it shows us that God left the Philistines in the land to test a generation who hadn't been tested in battle as yet. I know that sometimes we feel like we have already been tested in battle, yet God still leaves the 'Philistines' in our land.

If we look at what the Philistines mean, one interpretation of that is "to wallow." When things don't seem to be going quite right, sometimes we feel like we want to *wallow* where that testing is happening, where the Philistines are in our land. God says that He left them there to test us. If you feel like you have been tested today, or this week, or this month, or this year, know that that testing is God's purpose and provision for us. We are tested so that we might be winners of the battle.

As we see in Judges 3, it may be encouraging to know that no matter what happened, even when the Israelites were disobedient, or there was evil in the land, or evil in the camp, God still sent deliverers. In speaking of one of those deliverers, Shamgar, the scripture says, After Ehud came Shamgar son of Anath, who struck down six hundred Philistines with an oxgoad. He, too, saved Israel (Judges 3:31). (an oxgoad is a farm tool to prod or poke working animals (such as oxen) in their tasks, which may include plowing or moving into a corral). A modern version of an oxgoad that may be more familiar is a "cattle prod." This says to me that God will provide whatever we need. He will deliver us from the hand of the enemy, from the hands of evil, from the hands of our attackers. Yes, we truly are being delivered each day. As we know, Jesus is our great Deliverer.

It is true Satan's power has been broken in the death of Christ, but it has not yet been entirely set aside. The day will come when Satan will be bound and cast into the bottomless pit, but until then, the *Philistines* are among us, and God will allow this power at times to chasten His people, as He has done down through the ages. In the modern vernacular, the 'Philistine' is a person who is guided by materialism and is usually disdainful of the things of God. The 'Philistine' is used as a derogatory term, describing a person who is narrow-minded and hostile to the life of those who are in Christ. But the day is coming when the deliverance that Jesus accomplished on the cross for us will be fully actualized, and the 'Philistines' among us are chained and cast into utter darkness.

Chapter 5

The Flesh Versus the Spirit

Of all the judges in the Book of Judges, Samson is perhaps the most famous. Who can forget his miraculous birth, long hair, and feats of great strength? At Lehi, Samson became judge over Israel in the full sense of the word and testified to Israel concerning the truth. But the people had not received him. They were content to continue under the dominion of the Philistines, and when Samson began to oppose and offend the Philistines, they saw him only as a troublemaker and a disturber of their peace. Even when the Spirit of the Lord came upon Samson so that he wrought miraculous works of judgment against the Philistines, and the Philistines began to fear him greatly, the Israelites remained unimpressed.

When finally, the Philistines moved into their territory with a large army, determined to do away with Samson's interference, the Israelites were ready to help them. With three thousand men, they went to the rock Etam, and, taking Samson, they delivered him bound into the hands of their oppressors. It was then that the change took place. While they watched, the Spirit of God came upon Samson, and he broke apart the new ropes with which he had been bound as though they were old and seared by a fire.

As he approached Lehi, the Philistines came toward him shouting. The Spirit of the LORD came powerfully upon him. The ropes on his arms became like charred flax, and the bindings dropped from his hands. Finding a fresh jawbone of a donkey, he grabbed it and struck down a thousand men (Judges 15:14-15).

That night in the houses of Israel there was much soul-searching that took place. They had seen the Spirit of God working and could no longer look upon Samson with their former cold contempt. They began to realize that Samson was indeed a deliverer sent to them by God. But this deliverer had "feet of clay." There was an interplay between Samson's sexuality and his spirituality that was ever so strong. At last, wearied by the failure of the men of Gaza to meet his challenge, a disappointed Samson gave in to his besetting weakness. Samson had always had the greatest difficulty coping with his sexual lusts. That was why he had allowed his exploits in Timnah to be marred by his marriage to a daughter of the heathen Philistines.

He was not alone in this weakness. We find many other children of God in the Scriptures, heroes of faith whose lives were marred in a similar way. It is just that in Samson, it is so distasteful because he allowed it to combine so closely with his greatest works of faith. The greatest of the children of God have always shown themselves to be far from perfect. Samson in Gaza turned into the house of a prostitute. The Scripture says;

Alvin Frank, M. Div.

One day, Samson went to Gaza, where he saw a prostitute. He went in to spend the night with her. The people of Gaza were told, "Samson is here!" So they surrounded the place and lay in wait for him all night at the city gate. They made no move during the night, saying, "At dawn, we'll kill him." (Judges 16:1-2)

The Scripture tells us, "*One day Samson went to Gaza.*" It doesn't say why he went. One can only speculate that he went there to survey the city and observe its strongholds. Perhaps, like the two spies in Joshua 2, who were sent out by Joshua to observe the land, Samson probably went with this same intention;

Then Joshua, son of Nun, secretly sent two spies from Shittim. "Go, look over the land," he said, "especially Jericho." So they went and entered the house of a prostitute named Rahab and stayed there. The king of Jericho was told, "Look! Some of the Israelites have come here tonight to spy out the land" (Joshua 2:1-2).

The difference between the two spies and Samson is that while the two spies only took refuge from the prostitute Rahab and sought protection, Samson went into the prostitute with the intention of spending the whole night with her. At this point, Samson put his true mission on the 'back burner' in order that he might satisfy his sexual desires for a night. Samson, who at this point in his life could be classified as a womanizer, has now gone through half of the night

42

in the arms of this prostitute. And like an insect that has been captured by a Venus flytrap, Samson has an epiphany.

Perhaps in a moment of reflection and confession and repentance, the Holy Spirit spoke to his heart, reminding him about his Nazarite vows and of his mission as a deliverer from the same people in whose arms he now finds himself. The puzzling thing about Samson is the way he so freely mixes his mission with his sexual passion. But God is a God of grace and compassion, who gives us not just a second chance but continues to forgive us when we stray from the path that he has mapped out for us. So, in that moment of contrition, as Samson lies there, his mission once again becomes crystal clear - God has raised him up to take the lead in delivering his people from the tyranny of the Philistine.

But Samson lay there only until the middle of the night. Then he got up and took hold of the doors of the city gate, together with the two posts, and tore them loose, bar and all. He lifted them to his shoulders and carried them to the top of the hill that faces Hebron (Judges 16:3).

It was then, at the midnight hour, that the unexpected happened. Samson came out of the prostitute's house and resumed his mission of deliverance. The Philistines who had been guarding the gate, and by this time had fallen asleep, not expecting Samson until the morning, must have been in a state of epistemic ambivalence when they awoke to find the gate missing. They did not know what to believe. Surely, Samson knew that at this hour, the gates of the city were closed and tightly barred. He could not expect to get out at this hour. How foolish could he be? But there was no hesitation in the steps of this Israelite deliverer as he moved toward the city gate. His steps were quick and without stopping, as though he knew exactly what he intended.

Even when he stood before the very gates themselves, he seemed undisturbed by their locks and heavy bars. Rather, he reached out and grasped them with his hands. He lifted them to his shoulders and carried them to the top of the hill that faces Hebron. At first glance, this would seem like a playful prank or a show of someone exhibiting their strength. But that wasn't the case. Samson, now full of the Holy Spirit and with a renewed sense of calling, removed the gates of the city. By the light of the morning sun, the city stood naked and exposed. This was Gaza, the might and the boast of the Philistine nation.

The Gates of Gaza

Samson, a Nazarite and a man anointed and commissioned by God, knows a bit about the significance of 'gates.' Gates played and continues to play a significant role in God's salvific history. The gate is often presented as a place of power and authority. In Genesis 22:17, God makes a covenant with Abraham and promises him that "his seed shall possess the gate of his enemies," implying military victory and authority over adversarial nations. The Gates of Gaza had stood under the attack of countless invading forces. The strength of the city was its walls, and the strength of the walls was its gates. Many a mighty army had tried to destroy them, and they had stood fast. But now, one man had lifted them to his shoulders and carried them off. This was Gaza, standing naked and exposed in the morning sun, without its gates, without its strength, without its boast.

And then, as though to make it more unbelievable still, the report came back; the gates had been found with posts and bars and all. They were not in a nearby field; they were not downward by the sea; they were up on the mountain at its very peak. An army could hardly retrieve them, but they had been brought there by only one man. Here was a sign to which the Philistines might well take note.

The gates represented the strength of their city; and moved by the Spirit of Israel's God, one man had carried them off alone. It could only mean that with all their armies and fortified towns, they were helpless before this mighty God. In one moment, God would root out their greatest strength and carry it far away. They would do well to turn from oppressing His people and repent. But these were the Philistines, and they would not.

In the ancient world of the Bible, the gates of a city were crucial to its defenses. Their destruction symbolized the destruction of the city. Do you recall the lament of the fall of Jerusalem in Lamentations? — *"Her gates have sunk into the ground; their bars he has broken and destroyed. Her king and her princes are exiled among the nations, the law is no more, and her prophets no longer find visions from the LORD"* (Lamentations 2:9).

But this is not the whole story. The real significance of the gates in this text is that God, through Samson, continues to be faithful to the promises he made to the Patriarchs. To Abraham, in Genesis 22:17, God promises, *"Your seed shall possess the gate of their enemies."* In this text, therefore, Samson is a picture of God's faithfulness to his covenant people, to do for them what they repeatedly fail to do for themselves—to possess the land and all of God's good promises.

The events of Judges 16:1-3 may be seen as a one-night stand in the life and adventures of Samson, but it had far greater significance than that. Rather, we see God working against the tide of *Israel's disobedience* to fulfill his promises. Samson goes to Gaza to do what Israel was failing to do—possess the land and eliminate its pagan inhabitants. Like all of the judges, Samson prepares us for the coming of a king.

In fact, a careful reflection on the Scriptures may surprise us to learn that Samson is styled as David's John the Baptist. There are a number of features that connect Samson and John the Baptist. Both were born to older, barren women, and both were Nazirites for life. Most importantly, however, both men prepared the people for the arrival of a great king. Samson began the final battle with the Philistines, but it was David in 1 Samuel 17 who slew their champion, Goliath and finally eliminated the threat of the Philistines from the land.

Most of us quite like the Samson character because we can identify with him. We may rationalize Samson as a sinner, and I am a sinner. If God can use Samson, then surely God can use me. In fact, we are probably attracted to a figure like Samson because we believe that Samson sinned in ways greater than most of us do. So if God could love and use someone as "sinful" as Samson was, then surely God can love and use someone like you and me.

But I wonder if this type of interpretation is correct. Do these biblical narratives exist only to make us feel better about ourselves, or is there something more to this story? Did the author of the book of Hebrews include Samson in the "Hall of Faith" (Hebrews 11:32) because of his value for our self-esteem or because of the faithful execution of his office as judge—"*who by faith conquered kingdoms, administered justice, and gained what was promised*" (Hebrews. 11:33)?

Indeed, Samson was an imperfect man, as imperfect as all of us. But we should take no consolation in his imperfection or in

God's grace to bestow mercy. Each one of us is called by God to do a specific work and we have to determine in our hearts to be faithful. But most of the time, determination alone is not enough. When Samson took the vow of the Nazarite, he was determined to be obedient and serve the Lord his God. But he failed in many areas of his life.

The apostle Paul reminds us that we are imperfect people who, in spite of our best intentions and ardent desires, continue to fail. After looking at the struggle between the flesh and the spirit, he remains perplexed and cannot understand why he does what he does. For what he wants to do, he does not do, but what he hates, that he does.

Paul writes;

For I do not do the good I want to do, but the evil I do not want to do—this I keep on doing. Now if I do what I do not want to do, it is no longer I who do it, but it is sin living in me that does it. So I find this law at work: Although I want to do good, evil is right there with me. For in my inner being, I delight in God's law, but I see another law at work in me, waging war against the law of my mind and making me a prisoner of the law of sin at work within me. What a wretched man I am! Who will rescue me from this body that is subject to death? Thanks be to God, who delivers me through Jesus Christ our Lord! (Romans 7:19-25)

Jesus delivers us, not because we are strong, but because we abide or remain in him. Jesus says in John 15,

"*I am the vine; you are the branches. If you remain in me and I in you, you will bear much fruit; apart from me, you can do nothing. If you do not remain in me, you are like a branch that is thrown away and withers; such branches are picked up, thrown into the fire and burned*" (John 15:5-6).

Chapter 6
Trifling with the Spirit of God
The Holy Spirit

There are many misconceptions about the identity of the Holy Spirit. Some view the Holy Spirit as a mystical force. Others see the Holy Spirit as an impersonal power that God makes available to followers of Christ. What does the Bible say about the identity of the Holy Spirit? Simply put, the Bible declares that the Holy Spirit is God. The Bible also tells us that the Holy Spirit is a divine person, a being with a mind, emotions, and a will. No, the Holy Spirit is not a twenty-first-century phenomenon. Way back in the book of Genesis, we read, *"In the beginning, God created the heavens and the earth. Now the earth was formless and empty, darkness was over the surface of the deep, and the Spirit of God was hovering over the waters"* (Genesis 1:1-2).

In the Old Testament, God filled some of his servants with his Holy Spirit and empowered them for service. At that time, God filled particular people, at particular times, for particular tasks. The Holy Spirit came upon prophets, warriors, and judges such as Gideon. In Judges 13:25, we read; The Holy Spirit came upon Samson as well. "And the Spirit of the Lord began to stir him while he lived in Mahaneh-dan, which is located between the towns of Zorah and Eshtaol." The Holy Spirit enabled his servants to do great exploits as well as tell forth the message of the Lord. But the Holy Spirit is not limited to those Old Testament saints. God promised to fill all those who call upon him and believe in his name; *"I will give you a new heart and put a new spirit in you; I will remove from you your heart of stone and give you a heart of flesh. And I will put my Spirit in you and move you to follow my decrees and be careful to keep my laws"* (Ezekiel 36:26-27).

The work of the Spirit of God relates directly to the grace of God. It is impossible to walk in the grace of God without the work of the Spirit of God. Whenever the Spirit of God is at work in us, it is the grace of God that is being provided. The word of the Lord to His people was, "So he said to me, "This is the word of the LORD to Zerubbabel: '*Not by might nor by power, but by my Spirit,'* says *the LORD Almighty* (Zechariah 4:6). The Holy Spirit must be the dynamic agent in the work of building our lives – the temple of the Lord. This Scripture references a time when Zerubbabel was leading the people back from captivity into the Promised Land so that they would rebuild the temple of God. This act was to be done not by the might and power of man but by the work of the Holy Spirit.

In Zerubbabel's day, the task of rebuilding God's temple seemed to be like a great mountain because of the hostile and alien environment. Yet, this was not a threat to God. The word of the Lord to Zerubbabel was that this mountain would become a plain. It would become a flat place to march across when God was through with His task. And then ultimately, Zerubbabel would bring out the capstone - the last stone for the temple. With that final piece set in place, the only proper response that explained the whole work of God building the temple was to recognize God's grace.

The same may be said in regard to our lives. We must be built by the work of the Holy Spirit. When that last piece is put in place in our lives and in the life of the church before she is raptured, the only thing that can be said about that process is "Grace, grace to it!" Because out of the fullness of Jesus Christ, we have all received grace in place of grace already given. That is the way God works in our lives. He works by grace. Of His fullness we have all received, grace upon grace. So whenever we presume upon God's grace or trifle with His Spirit, we are treading on unholy ground.

Grieve not the Holy Spirit.

We can grieve the Holy Spirit in several ways: when we presume upon his grace, take his love and grace for granted, ignore his promptings to have our lives transformed or, in the case of Samson, become so spiritually desensitized that we are unaware that the Lord has left us. Ephesians 4:30 gives us a fair warning; *"And do not grieve the Holy Spirit of God, with whom you were sealed for the day of redemption."*

Growing up, my understanding of God's grace was somewhat skewed. I vaguely understood that God loved me and that he sent Jesus to die for me. I understood that as a result of what he did, I was supposed to stop doing bad things and only do good things. But I believed that if I did bad things, it would be okay because God would forgive me. I presumed that God would always forgive me no matter how sinfully I lived. I could live as I wanted, ask God for forgiveness later, and be assured that somehow God would be there for me. In essence, what I thought I had was a license to get away with all the 'fun stuff' and still have the embrace of God in my life! In my arrogance, I presumed that God needed to forgive me since I was following the system: sin, pray for forgiveness, be forgiven, repeat…

Later, I realized that this understanding of God's grace was incongruent with the gospel message, as it cheapened God's grace and took God for granted. But there is nothing new under the sun. The Bible gives plenty of examples of people presuming upon God's grace. In Numbers 14, Israel, being distraught over a bad report from the 10 spies, decides to disobey God and not enter into the Promised Land as God had commanded. When Moses tells them of God's judgment because of their disobedience, they "repent". Presuming that God would honor their admittance of sin, they decide to enter the land as originally instructed. But by then, God was not with them, and they were defeated by their enemies.

In Jeremiah 7, the prophet Jeremiah is warning Judah that their idolatry will be judged by God and that they need to repent in order to be saved. But they made the Temple into "a den of robbers," a safe haven from God's judgment no matter how sinfully they lived. Judah presumed that God's judgment would never extend to His own Temple, and so they would be safe in Jerusalem. This type of presumption of the Lord can also be seen in the New Testament. In Matthew 3, John the Baptist calls out the Pharisees and Sadducees for their superficial religiosity and misplaced hope in their ancestry. John explains to them that their sinful hearts were not going to be overlooked simply because they were sons of Abraham. True decedents of Abraham need to share his extraordinary obedience and faith.

The Apostle Paul warns the Romans not to presume upon God's grace in Romans 2. He tells them that judging another person's sins while committing the same sins invites God's judgment upon the one who is judging. He goes on to explain that for them to "presume on the riches of God's kindness, forbearance and patience" is the opposite of what God desires - repentance. In all these examples, we see people presuming upon God's grace, using it as an excuse to sin rather than a motivation for true repentance.

They were living in a form of cheap grace and continual sin, which Paul addresses in Romans 6. In that chapter, Paul, anticipating the arguments from the religious establishment against salvation by grace alone, unequivocally denounces the idea that one can be saved and keeps on living a sinful life. In verses 1 and 2, he states, *"What shall we say, then? Shall we go on sinning so that grace may increase? By no means! We are those who have died to sin; how can we live in it any longer?"* (Romans 6:1-2). And again, in verse 15, he says, *"What then? Shall we sin because we are not under the law but under grace? By no means!"* (Romans 6:15).

The Bible is clear that we serve a loving, gracious and merciful God, but that doesn't mean we can do whatever we want without consequence. In order to avoid the trap of presuming upon God's grace, Christians must live a life that shows Christ to be Lord and not only as Savior.

Through Scripture, we can know God and his will for us. Failing to show evidence of a changed heart through an obedient life will result in unwelcome consequences. Christ himself said, *"Not everyone who says to me, 'Lord, Lord,' will enter the kingdom of heaven, but only the one who does the will of my Father who is in heaven. Many will say to me on that day, 'Lord, Lord, did we not prophesy in your name and in your name drive out demons, and in your name perform many miracles?' Then I will tell them plainly, 'I never knew you. Away from me, you evildoers!"* (Matthew 7:21-23).

Alvin Frank, M. Div.

The people in the above examples were not going to be saved by their admission of guilt, proximity to God's house, birthright or misguided understanding of God's kindness. True salvation comes from an accurate understanding of the cost required to save and the cost required to be saved. Those who are saved will exhibit a changed heart that loves God, which in turn results in a holy life. We show our love and obedience by the way we respond to the word of God; *"If you love me, keep my commands"* (John 14:15). So even though Samson was called by God and consecrated by him before he was born and received the Holy Spirit's anointing at a very early age, he had to keep on living by the Spirit and not by the flesh, if he wanted to be victorious in his mission.

Do Not Ignore the Promptings of the Holy Spirit

When the Lord, through his Holy Spirit, presents evidence upon evidence and brings the light of Jesus to a person's awareness, why is it that people hesitate to walk in that light? By every hesitation and delay, one places himself or herself where it is more and more difficult to accept the light of heaven, and at last it seems impossible to be impressed by admonitions and warnings. The spiritual offender says, more and more easily, as was said in the book of Acts by Felix, with whom the apostle Paul was sharing the good news of the Gospel. *Several days later, Felix came with his wife, Drusilla, who was Jewish. He sent for Paul and listened to him as he spoke about faith in Christ Jesus. As Paul talked about*

56

righteousness, self-control and the judgment to come, Felix was afraid and said, "That's enough for now! You may leave. When I find it convenient, I will send for you." (Acts 24: 24-25).

The person who is drawn again and again by the Spirit of the Lord, and who slights the warnings given, does not yield to his convictions to repent or to change the direction of his/her life, and who does not heed the exhortation to seek pardon and grace, is in a perilous position. Jesus is drawing him, the Spirit is exerting His power upon him, urging him to surrender his will to the will of God, and when this invitation is unheeded, the Spirit is grieved and ceases to further entreat. After all this, if the sinner chooses to remain in sin and impenitence, although he/she has evidence to encourage his/her faith, no more evidence would do any good. That person is being drawn by another to whom he is responding, and that is the drawing of Satan. That person yields obedience to the powers of darkness. This, of course, is fatal and leaves the soul in obstinate impenitence.

This is the blasphemy that is most general among those who reject the prompting of the Holy Spirit. This works in a most subtle way until the sinner feels no more remorse of conscience, no repentance, and consequently has no pardon. Those who resist the Spirit of God think that they will repent at some future day when they get ready to take a decided step toward reformation, but repentance will then be beyond their power. So whatever you do, never, never feel at liberty to trifle with the opportunities granted to you by the Holy Spirit. Study the will of God; do not study how you can avoid keeping the commandments of God, but study rather how you may keep them in sincerity and truth and truly serve Him whose property you are.

As was mentioned in the 'Introduction of this book', Samson in the Valley of Sorek exemplifies so accurately what a diver experiences in the deep - feelings that are similar to mild alcohol intoxication - this is the result of nitrogen narcosis. Similarly, the spiritual desensitization Samson is experiencing is brought about by his constant neglect of the Holy Spirit's promptings. Like the diver, Samson feels very much at home in an environment that is totally foreign to his true calling and one that can prove fatal at a moment's notice. He basks almost playfully as a dolphin frolicking in the deep. But in this state of euphoria, as he enjoys the ride of these strange undercurrents, they can eventually take him to his death.

As a follower of Jesus, we, too are living in a foreign environment. The Scriptures tell us that we are 'strangers and pilgrims' in this world. And if we are not careful, we too can be lulled into a state of euphoria, where this hostile environment begins to dictate the standards by which we ought to live. The Bible tells us that these things are written for our example, giving us warning so that we do not fall into the same snares that they experienced; *"Therefore, since we are surrounded by such a great cloud of witnesses, let us throw off everything that hinders and the sin that so easily entangles. And let us run with perseverance the race marked out for us, fixing our eyes on Jesus, the pioneer and perfecter of faith. For the joy set before him he endured the cross, scorning its shame, and sat down at the right hand of the throne of God*" (Hebrews 12:1-2).

Presumption by Disobedience

God and His word are not to be trifled with. The story is found in 1 Chronicles 13. King David desired, above all else, to bring the Ark of the Covenant to Jerusalem. Now the Ark, or what is also known as God's mercy seat (Exodus 25:17), was a representation of God presence on earth (Exodus 25:22). This is brought out in 1 Chronicles 13:6. "*David and all Israel went to Baalah of Judah (Kiriath Jearim) to bring up from there the Ark of God the LORD, who is enthroned between the cherubim—the Ark that is called by the Name.*" However, instead of the priest carrying the Ark as revealed in the Scriptures (Exodus 25:14; 1 Chronicles 15:2, 12-15), David decided to put the Ark on a new cart and pull it with a team of oxen.

In David's mind, he and his men were honoring God, especially in their worshipping God as the Ark proceeded to its designation (1 Chronicles 13:8). As a result, God struck Uzzah when he stretched out his hand to steady and protect the Ark from falling (1 Chronicles 13:9-11). God is holy, and we are to honor that holiness in the way we treat the things of God and, more specifically, God's word by living our lives in accordance with it. What I see is that we can do all sorts of seemingly good things to show our love for God, including religious things, but if we are not doing it according to God's way as outlined in God's word, then it's all for naught. *"Does the Lord delights in burnt offerings and sacrifices as much as in obeying the Lord? To obey is better than sacrifice, and to heed is better than the fat of rams"* (1 Samuel 15:22).

It's not that God didn't want to be honored and for His presence to be brought into the midst of His people's everyday life. He just wanted to be honored His way through the people's obedience. What David experienced firsthand was that the presence of a Holy God is not something to be trifled with. Similarly, we may look at Samson's many adventures on the wild side and think because God eventually used them to destroy the enemy, that Samson could be exonerated. However, for God's own glory and because of his love for his children, He will sometimes use even our missteps in order to accomplish his purposes.

Presumption by Familiarity

There are times when we can become so familiar with the Holy Spirit that we take for granted that we can do no wrong and that if we do, it will be overlooked because we have become *buddy-buddy* with the Holy Spirit. There are many examples in the

Scriptures about this. But the one that comes to mind is the presumptuousness of King Uzziah, 2 Chronicles 26.

Following the death of his father, Amaziah, who was assassinated by his people, Uzziah was made king at a very early age.

> Uzziah was sixteen years old when he became king, and he reigned in Jerusalem for fifty-two years. His mother's name was Jekoliah; she was from Jerusalem. He did what was right in the eyes of the LORD, just as his father Amaziah had done. He sought God during the days of Zechariah, who instructed him in the fear of God. As long as he sought the LORD, God gave him success. He went to war against the Philistines and broke down the walls of Gath, Jabneh and Ashdod. He then rebuilt towns near Ashdod and elsewhere among the Philistines. God helped him against the Philistines against the Arabs who lived in Gur Baal, and against the Meunites. The Ammonites brought tribute to Uzziah, and his fame spread as far as the border of Egypt because he had become very powerful (2 Chronicles 26:3-8).

Uzziah was very industrious, and he built many fortified places in Jerusalem. And he had a well-trained army, ready to go out by divisions when needed. In Jerusalem he made devices invented to be used on the towers and on the corner defenses so that soldiers could shoot arrows and hurl large stones from the walls. His fame spread far and wide, for he was greatly helped until he became powerful. He had become very strong with God's help.

> But after Uzziah became powerful, his pride led to his downfall. He was unfaithful to the LORD his God and entered the temple of the LORD to burn incense on the altar of incense. Azariah, the priest, with eighty other courageous priests of the LORD, followed him in. They confronted King Uzziah and said, "It is not right for you, Uzziah, to burn incense to the LORD. That is for the priests, the descendants of Aaron, who have been consecrated to burn incense. Leave the sanctuary, for you have been unfaithful, and you will not be honored by the LORD God." (2 Chronicles 26: 16-18).

Unfortunately, Uzziah's familiarity with the grace of God and the help that he had received from God had made him take for granted the holiness of God. He had become so great in his own eyes that he couldn't see the folly of his ways in usurping the office of the priest, dishonoring the temple of God, by burning incense to 'his buddy' – the Lord.

> Uzziah, who had a censer in his hand, ready to burn incense, became angry. While he was raging at the priests in their presence before the incense altar in the LORD's temple, leprosy broke out on his forehead. When Azariah, the chief priest and all the other priests looked at him, they saw that he had leprosy on his forehead, so they hurried him out. Indeed, he himself was eager to leave because the LORD had afflicted him (2 Chronicles 26:19-20).

The Scriptures go on to tell us that King Uzziah had leprosy until the day he died. He lived in a separate house—a leprous man and banned from the temple of the LORD. Leprosy in the Bible is synonymous with sin. And so, this powerful king, who at an early age was blessed and anointed by the Lord – a man who had accomplished many great things, not by his own strength or ability but truly by the Lord, lived out the rest of his life with the mark of sin on his forehead, because when he became powerful, his familiarity with the grace of God led to pride, which became his downfall.

Perhaps at this point, you may be thinking, as you look back over your life, that you are no different than Uzziah. You may be thinking, "It's too late for me. I may have begun well, but I'm finishing poorly. I have a track record of sins that disqualify me from being able to say I will finish well." But that's not where I wish to leave you as we come to the end of this chapter. For in Christ, there always remains the opportunity to finish well. Praise God! The power of repentance and forgiveness that Christ offers can restore a man or a woman so profoundly that their sinful nature, which may have spelled ruin, can be redeemed.

Think for a moment about King David. Truly, we would have concluded that with his adultery with Bathsheba and his murder of Uriah, he was finished. But David repented. His prayer of repentance is preserved for us in Psalm 51 summed up in these three verses; *"Create in me a pure heart, O God, and renew a steadfast spirit within me. Do not cast me from your presence or take your Holy Spirit from me. Restore to me the joy of your salvation and grant me a willing spirit, to sustain me"* (Psalm 51:10-12). Along with his prayer of restoration, summed up in these two verses in Psalm 32, David encourages our heart; *"Blessed is the one whose transgressions are forgiven, whose sins are covered. Blessed is the one whose sin the LORD does not count against them and in whose spirit is no deceit"* (Psalm 23:1-2). In all of this, David is remembered as a man after God's own heart.

Think also of the apostle Peter, who denied Christ publicly three times in the crucial hours of Christ's suffering and death, the ultimate treachery. And yet, we know from John 21 that Christ restored Peter, and he became among the most effective of the apostles. And if David and Peter aren't convincing enough, then I point you to the thief on the cross beside the Lord Jesus. In his dying hours, the thief repented and believed in Christ and was that very day with Christ in paradise, and that is how that criminal whose crimes deserved death on the cross, is remembered. He finished well. And so, if you are among those who wonder if you have any hope of finishing well, let me assure you: Christ has made that possible. He's only asking that you return to Him, confess your sins, and be forgiven. And that, my dear friend, in the final analysis, is true for every one of us.

Prayer

Heavenly Father, thank you for this important warning and lesson from the life and the reign of King Uzziah. Father, we have much in common with him. We often forget to remember the countless ways You have provided for us, protected us, and demonstrated Your favor. Instead of gratitude leading to faithfulness, our hearts migrate to pride and discontent that render us more often than we want to admit, living in the flesh without thought for You. Thank you as well for the remedy of repentance and forgiveness that is ours in Christ. Help us to become competent in repentance, Father, that we may indeed finish this life well for Your glory. We ask it in Jesus' name. Amen.

Chapter 7
The Valley of Sorek

After Samson's escapades in Gaza, where he removed the gates of the city and took it to the top of a hill looking towards Hebron, the Philistines, who were left embarrassed, angry and vulnerable, sought ways to capture and kill him. But Samson, who, psychologically, may be classified as a womanizer with a weakness toward women of ill repute, soon becomes a pawn in the hands of someone with whom he thinks he has fallen in love. Her name was Delilah, meaning "delicate" or "(she who) weakened."

In Judges 16:4-5, we read;

Sometime later, he fell in love with a woman in the Valley of Sorek whose name was Delilah. The rulers of the Philistines went to her and said, "See if you can lure him into showing you the secret of his great strength and how we can overpower him so we may tie him up and subdue him. Each one of us will give you eleven hundred shekels (about 13 kilograms) of silver." (Judges 16:4-5)

The Valley of Sorek

The Valley of Sorek is west of Jerusalem. The name of this location is supposedly related to a specific type of grape. We are not told exactly where this valley was located, but we know it was a valley that separated the Land of Judah from the Philistines. The name is a subtle foreshadowing of Samson's impending disobedience: If you recall, Samson was meant to live as a Nazirite (Judges 13:4–5). That vow required total abstinence from all grapes and grape products. In this valley, he will finally encounter a temptation that neither his cleverness nor strength can overcome.

Samson has fallen for another woman in this territory, though the actual name of the specific town is not given. When Samson was involved with other women, Scripture noted only that he "saw" them (Judges 14:1; 16:1). This corresponds to his uncontrolled, lustful urges. Now, however, the Bible says Samson "loved" a woman. His connection to her is deeper than mere attraction. As the rest of this passage shows, he is vulnerable and honest with her. What would otherwise be a good sign and a step of maturity will be the last and most disastrous mistake of Samson's life.

Samson in the Valley of Sorek is a metaphor for those forbidden places and forbidden adventures that the children of God usually embark upon, usually in disobedience to the word of God, only to find themselves in great distress and needing to be rescued by the gracious hand of God. Samson possessed supernatural strength from God (Judges 14:5–6, 19; 15:14–15; 16:3). Yet he never overcame the mundane, common weakness of many men: an insatiable appetite for women, usually women of ill repute. This weak point of his, will be fully exploited by Delilah and her Philistine sponsors, leading to Samson's eventual capture and death.

Metaphorically speaking, the Valley of Sorek is that beckoning gate that leads to the house of the enemy. It is that rope called pleasure that is tied to our waist, pulling us back to the things we do not want to do. The Valley of Sorek is that place where good and evil meet and the good is corrupted by evil. It is that place that looks good on the outside but it is a place of bitter and constant regrets. Sorek is a place of separation. It is a place where God's presence will never go with us - a place where God gave instructions never to go. The Valley of Sorek is that cleverly concealed sin we are committing, thinking and hoping nobody will see us. Sorek is that place we visit in the dark, foolishly thinking God does not see us.

As we take a closer look at the Valley of Sorek, where those forbidden grapes are grown, we see it as a spiritual and physical pollution that is pushing heaven away from us. It is that *friend* that makes us feel comfortable with sin, only to back out in laughter when we become trapped. Sorek is those less-than-wholesome shows or pictures we are bold enough to look at as we listen to that loud voice that tells us it doesn't matter, God understands. In the Valley of Sorek, there is that dark cloud that makes us feel we are being hidden from God, but instead, it blocks and separates our direct access to heaven.

Samson in the Valley of Sorek

Many times, when we feel like the heavens have become like brass and our prayers are returning to us unanswered, it is because we are in the Valley of Sorek. Sorek is that thing that drives God away and blocks our communication with Heaven. It makes us live in a state of spiritual laziness. The Valley of Sorek is that place where we listen and follow those 'ear-tickling' messages, not warning us about our sins but telling us about prosperity and grace. In the Valley of Sorek, there is that 'wasting power' that wastes the lives of young men and women. It is that place where the great are brought to nothing – where we 'tie God's hands' because of our sin and where the name of the Lord is brought into ridicule.

So Delilah said to Samson, "Tell me the secret of your great strength and how you can be tied up and subdued." (Judges 16:5)

Sometimes in our imagination, we see Samson as the mythological figure named *Hercules*. We see him standing head and shoulders above everyone, with bulging muscles and abs of steel. But this is not the case. No one ever asked Hercules for *the secret of his great strength.* The source of his great strength would have been obvious. If Samson, in the Valley of Sorek, had been all rippling muscles, Delilah would not have had to ask where his strength lay. His strength was from God, not from his muscles. And yet he would've been perceived as a "real man," a strong man. It was just enigmatic to everyone how this was when an ordinary man acted so strong.

So Delilah, the final and deadliest woman in Samson's life with great deception, pretends to love Samson in return. Her name has become synonymous with lust, deceit, betrayal and ruin. With much prodding, she tries to find the secret of his strength for an enormous bribe offered to her. So Delilah said to Samson, *"Tell me the secret of your great strength and how you can be tied up and subdued"* (Judges 16:6).

On three previous occasions, Samson tricked Delilah into believing that the source of his strength was in his own body and that if he were bound in various ways, then he would become as weak as any other man. But on each occasion, when Delilah said to him, "Samson, the Philistines are upon you!" He snapped the bindings that held him as easily as a piece of string snaps when it came close to a flame. This deception infuriated Delilah to no end!

> Then she said to him, "How can you say, 'I love you,' when you don't confide in me? This is the third time you have made a fool of me and haven't told me the secret of your great strength." With such nagging, she prodded him day after day until he was sick to death of it. So he told her everything. "No razor has ever been used on my head," he said, "because I have been a Nazirite dedicated to God from my mother's womb. If my head were shaved, my strength would leave me, and I would become as weak as any other

man" (Judges 16:15-17). So she finally wears him down.

At last, he falls into the hands of Delilah. He falls asleep on her lap – the lap of the enemy. He foolishly plays with his own destruction. At last, he lets out the secret, and his strength lay in his locks. Not that his hair made him strong, but that his hair was the symbol of his consecration and was the pledge of God's favor to him.

When Delilah saw that he had told her everything, she sent word to the rulers of the Philistines, "Come back once more; he has told me everything." So, the rulers of the Philistines returned with the silver in their hands. After putting him to sleep on her lap, she called for someone to shave off the seven braids of his hair and so began to subdue him. And his strength left him (Judges 16:18-19).

While his hair was untouched, he was a consecrated man, but as soon as that was cut away, he was no longer perfectly consecrated, and then his strength departed from him.

Then she called, "Samson, the Philistines are upon you!" He awoke from his sleep and thought, "I'll go out as before and shake myself free." But he did not know that the LORD had left him (Judges 16:20).

This statement in the book of Judges about Samson is one of the saddest portions of Scripture in the Bible. *"I'll go out as before and shake myself free." But he did not know that the LORD had left him.*

This is Samson, the Nazarite. The one whom the Holy Spirit stirred at a very early age, the one on whom the Holy Spirit came on so many occasions, and in whom he was able to do so many great exploits. *He did not know that the Lord had left him.* How does one get to such a place where they are no longer aware of God's presence or absence? I believe it happens when we presume on God's grace, taking it for granted, mistaking his kindness and his patience as a license to immoral living. This usually results in a downward spiral that leads to death.

Becoming Spiritually Desensitized

Becoming spiritually desensitized does not come through a giant leap but through tinny steps in a direction from which there is usually no return. Most of the time, it does not come with a wilful or conscious stepping away from that which we know to be true but with a gradual wandering that leads to entrapment. The 'Valley of Sorek' is that place where we find ourselves after ignoring the subtle and sometimes not-so-subtle prodding by the Holy Spirit to change course, usually to turn around.

Samson in the Valley of Sorek

We usually find ourselves in the 'Valley of Sorek' when we despise our consecration to the Lord, trampling it underfoot as we allow the lust of sinful nature to propel us to a place where we can satisfy our carnal desires. When we do, we are leaving ourselves unprotected by the divine covering of the Lord and open to the devices of Satan. The 'Valley of Sorek' is that place in which we find ourselves after the willful neglect of the word of God, which is intended to be our guide and moral compass.

When we ignore the decrees of the Lord, we begin to walk in step with the wicked and stand in the way that sinners take. We no longer delight ourselves in the law of the LORD or meditate on his word by day or night. When we ignore God's word, we sever our connection with the 'True Vine', and our leaves begin to wither, as it says in Psalm 1. We become like the chaff that the wind blows away. For the LORD watches over the way of the righteous, but the way of the one who wilfully strays leads to destruction.

Samson, at this juncture, fully devoid of the presence of the Holy Spirit but totally unaware of it, thinks that he would be able to free himself as before. However, this time, he is on his own. He is 'running on empty', as the saying goes. *"Then the Philistines seized him, gouged out his eyes and took him down to Gaza. Binding him with bronze shackles, they set him to grinding grain in the prison. But the hair on his head began to grow again after it had been shaved* (Judges 16:21-22).

73

Alvin Frank, M. Div.

His hair is cut away, his eyes are gouged out, and he was taken to Gaza, where the Philistines began to oppress him. How has the mighty fallen!

Yes, now he is brought back to the very city out of which he had walked in all his pride with the gates and bolts upon his shoulders. He has become a spectacle and a laughingstock. Every passer-by, including the little children, would come out to mock him. The crowds of people would come around him and point at him – "Samson, the great hero, has fallen! Let us make sport of him!" What a spectacle. Why, he must be the sport and jest of every passer-by, who will step in to see this great wonder – the destroyer of the Philistines - now made to toil at the mill.

This picture of disdain and ridicule is one with which we have become too familiar in our day, as many who have done great exploits in the name of the Lord have become laughingstocks by the enemies of Jesus Christ. Many have left the ministry in disgrace because in their desire to make a name for themselves and build great empires, rather than the kingdom of God, '*did not know that the Lord had left them*'. Some, like Samson, have found forgiveness from a merciful God. Others, however, may have ended up in prison, while still others have had their misdeeds follow them to the grave.

That Samson should have lost his eyes was terrible; that he should have lost his strength was worse; but that he should have lost the favor of God for a while - that he should become the sport of God's enemies was the worst of all. Samson's soiled life is recorded for all to see. His defeats are clear and unvarnished. They speak to us regarding the practice of sin, which blinds us and then slowly binds us with its fetters. Finally, blinded and bound, we have to go grinding through life, full of guilt and shame, because of sin. But we serve a merciful God who is very quick to forgive when we recognize our sins and disobedience and call out to him to deliver us.

Talk to anybody that's lived an immoral life that's come to Christ - ask them how exciting it really was. Talk to someone who's been in the drug culture that's come to Christ - ask them whether it's as exciting as it appears to be in the media. Talk to anybody who's gotten into the world of alcohol bars. Talk to anyone who has lived a life of sexual perversion and promiscuity, and ask them whether it really satisfies them. It doesn't - it has a passing pleasure that slowly blinds - that binds us with cords that we forge for ourselves - that we cannot break, and finally, we become the one who is grinding out an existence, living as a captive of sin. But God forgives, God restores, and God uses Samson one final time.

The greatest enemy Samson had was himself. What a warning to each of us who have the same problem—it is called our flesh. Within each of us, a traitorous inclination against God never slumbers and always smolders. Given any amount of fuel either through the desires of the body, the desires of the eyes or the pride of life—and it blazes to life in a conflagration of destruction. Samson's history is an illustration of Paul's warning in 1 Corinthians 9;

"No, I strike a blow to my body and make it my slave so that after I have preached to others, I myself will not be disqualified for the prize" (1 Corinthians 9:27).

In Heaven, among the spiritual heroes, Samson is remembered as a man of faith. On earth, he is remembered as a man whose strength was in God but who was weak in his flesh. Hebrews 11:32 cites him for his faith in God's word: *And what more shall I say? I do not have time to tell about Gideon, Barak, Samson and Jephthah, about David and Samuel and the prophets, who through faith conquered kingdoms, administered justice, and gained what was promised; who shut the mouths of lions* (Hebrews 11:32).

Of all the biblical characters, Samson was one that we may describe as the one whose "wheels" totally came off along his Journey with the Lord. As we read his story, we will see that he was mostly 'out of control.' In many ways, he epitomizes a kind of rugged "man's man" in our culture today (brut strength, a womanizer, independent, even violent). But in the end, his story is tragic. He ends up stripped of his God-given abilities, blinded, and bound, and only to die with God's help, as with one final 'push' destroyed 3000 Philistines in his death. Such is the destructive bent of one who disregards God's commands and presumes on God's grace.

So, what are some lessons we may learn from Samson's life?

1. **Our true measure is not found in our physical strength or appearance.**

Samson seems to be a man in search of his identity. Even his strength and ability to overpower (both men and women) did not bring any sense of peace to Samson's life. Our worth is found in Christ, what He's already said about us and what He's already done for us.

2. **We cannot trust in our strength; it can become our greatest weakness.**

It is possible to squander the very gifts God has given you to live out his purposes for your life. Failure to give those gifts fully over to God will carry a high price tag. Samson's strength became his demise. He did not use his God-given strength for God alone. He used it to leverage his own desires.

3. **Strength in one area of your life does not make up for weakness in another.**

We must live our lives in balance, honoring God as well as loving and respecting others. We may be "successful" in certain areas of our lives and still fail where it matters most.

4. **We must acknowledge our weakness before God.**

Admit where we are most apt to fall. Name it; say it out loud and tell others. Sin unconfessed is sin revisited. Sin revisited is a sin that is self-destructive.

5.   There are always consequences for disobedience.

Samson's story goes from sad to tragic when he does not learn from his mistakes. He repeats the same bad mistake of entering into relationships with sinful women. So guys, Watch out for Delilahs. Girls: Watch out for guys like Samson. You must guard your heart!

6.   God can restore us for His purposes even after we fall.

Though we may face the consequences of our sins for the rest of our lives, God can restore us and use us for his glory.

Samson's story is a warning against pride and taking for granted the blessings that God has given us. It can often be easy to stray, throwing off constraints - wanting our own way like Samson did. But his story reminds us of the dangers of disobeying God to follow our own desires. So, just as God still heard and answered Samson's final prayer despite his full-on sprint into destruction, he also hears us and will answer when we call Him, no matter how many times we've messed up.

However, most of the time, we have to come to grips with the fact that after we have repented and are forgiven by God, we may not enter back into a particular place or position as we previously had. But God will still accomplish His purposes through our life. Samson ended up in the "Hall of Faith" because he continued to believe in God - even in the end. So let us continue to trust in God and put NO confidence in the flesh. Because in the end, if we rely on our own strength, we will stumble and fall.

Isn't it amazing to know that, no matter what we have done or what went wrong, God is still willing and ready to give us a second chance? Remember Isaiah 1:18: *"Come now, let us settle the matter," says the LORD. "Though your sins are like scarlet, they shall be as white as snow; though they are red as crimson, they shall be like wool."*

Chapter 8
The Sin of Presumption

As the book of Judges progresses, we see more and more of the truth expressed in the last verse of the book coming into play – 'In those days there was no king in Israel; everyone did what was right in his own eyes.' We are even starting to see this in Samson's life, and He was God's deliverer! Does this not remind us of the Early Church age mentioned in Revelation – Laodicea, which means "the peoples' opinions" or "the people's rule." And do we not see this increasing when we look at the Western church as a whole today? Jesus isn't being enthroned as King, and even his (professed) people are starting to 'do what is right in their own eyes.'

In those days, Israel had no king; everyone did as they saw fit (Judges 21:25).

When one assumes or presumes that a certain action is permissible, based only on the thought that the relationship which exists between them and another gives them the right to proceed with that action, then that person is presuming on the grace or love of the other. When it comes to being presumptuous about the grace and mercy of God, the consequences can be grave. Nadab and Abihu assumed God would accept their incorrectly measured incense (Leviticus 10:1-2; Exodus 30:34).

Samson in the Valley of Sorek

Uzzah assumed God wouldn't mind if he kept the Ark from falling (2 Samuel 6:6-7); Israel assumed God would give them victory against the Philistines because of the Ark's presence (1 Samuel 4:3-11); Jewish businessmen assumed God would extend their lives another year to make money (James. 4:13-17); Uzziah assumed that because God had helped him to become strong, he was exempt from the prohibition of performing a duty in the temple, reserved only for the priest (2 Chronicles 26), et cetera. The casualty list reads like a phone book of the people who presumed God with dreadful consequences.

Every sin is rebellion against God, but presumption super-sizes the evil. When we come to Samson, we see how there are so many instances of him presuming on the grace and mercy of God. But the one that stands out the most is when he divulges the secret of his strength to the evil Delilah and falls asleep in her lap. After playing "Russian Roulette" with the grace of God on three separate occasions, by inventing ways in which his great strength may be sapped, he was about to get a rude awakening. On each occasion when Delilah would call out, "*Samson, the Philistines are upon you!*" He would then rise up and snap that with which he was bound, much to the dismay of his would-be captors. Thus, he managed to conceal the secret of his strength. This he did on three separate occasions.

But on the fourth occasion, the consequences of taking 'fire in one's lap' and expecting not to be burnt proved to be his undoing:

> Then she said to him, "How can you say, 'I love you,' when you don't confide in me? This is the third time you have made a fool of me and haven't told me the secret of your great strength." With such nagging she prodded him day after day until he was sick to death of it. So he told her everything. "No razor has ever been used on my head," he said, "because I have been a Nazirite dedicated to God from my mother's womb. If my head were shaved, my strength would leave me, and I would become as weak as any other man" (Judges 16:15-17).

"How can you say, 'I love you?'" It's a phrase that has deception written all over it. It reads like a spy novel when the protagonist is being duped by the beguiling traitor to divulge his secret. Samson, at this stage of his downward spiral in the process of being spiritually desensitized, is no longer able to discern truth from fiction. Like the metaphorical diver, Samson has been drifting slowly under the surface of the water, going deeper and deeper, until at this point of numbness, those strange undercurrents are sweeping him away.

When Delilah saw that he had told her everything, she sent word to the rulers of the Philistines, "Come back once more; he has told me everything." So, the rulers of the Philistines returned with the silver in their hands. After putting him to sleep on her lap, she called for someone to shave off the seven braids of his hair, and so began to subdue him. And his strength left him (Judges 16:18-19).

Samson had been more than once brought into mischief and danger by the 'love' of women, yet he would not take warning, but is again taken in the same snare, and this (recorded) third time is fatal. Licentiousness is one of the things that take away the heart. This is a deep pit into which many have fallen but from which few have escaped. And those who are fortunate, by a miracle of mercy, escape with the loss of reputation and usefulness of almost everything except their souls. They are soon to discover that the anguish of their suffering is ten thousand times greater than all the pleasures of sin.

Then she called, "Samson, the Philistines are upon you!" He awoke from his sleep and thought, "I'll go out as before and shake myself free." But he did not know that the LORD had left him (Judges 16:20).

He did not know

"I'll go out as before and shake myself free." To Samson, the Spirit of the Lord had become his servant, well so he must have thought. He had been given a 'magic wand' which he just needs to wave whenever he gets himself in trouble, then all will be well again. Well, Samson has miscalculated, misjudged and presumed, one time too many. Proverbs 29:1 says it quite clearly; "*Whoever remains stiff-necked after many rebukes will suddenly be destroyed—without remedy.*"

> Then the Philistines seized him, gouged out his eyes and took him down to Gaza. Binding him with bronze shackles, they set him to grinding grain in the prison (Judges 16:21).

The sin of presumption lies close beside the virtue of perfect faith and confidence in God. In the second temptation of Christ (Matthew 4:5-7), Satan flattered himself that he could take advantage of the humanity of Christ to lure Him over the line of trust to presumption. Lacking the ability to discern at this point, many souls are wrecked. Satan tried to deceive Christ through flattery. He then urged Christ to give him one more proof of His entire dependence upon God, one more evidence of His faith that He was the Son of God, by casting Himself from the Temple. He told Christ that if He were indeed the Son of God, He had nothing to fear, for angels were at hand to uphold Him. Satan gave evidence that he understood the Scriptures by the use he made of them, interpreting them conveniently.

But Jesus did not waver from His integrity and showed that He had perfect faith in His Father's promised care. He would not put the faithfulness and love of His Father to a needless trial, although He was in the presence of an enemy and placed in a position of extreme difficulty and peril. He would not, at Satan's suggestion, tempt God by presumptuously experimenting on His providence. Satan had quoted Scripture which seemed appropriate for the occasion, hoping to accomplish his designs. He made quite an appeal to the Lord at this special time but to no avail.

Christ knew that God could indeed bear Him up if He had required Him to throw Himself from the Temple. But to do this unbidden by the Father and to experiment with His protecting care and love because He was dared by Satan to do so would not have shown His strength of faith. Satan was well aware that if Christ could be prevailed upon to do something that the Father did not call Him to do – to fling Himself from the Temple to prove that His Father would protect Him – it would show the weakness of His human nature.

Christ came off victoriously in the second temptation, as well as the first and the third. He manifested perfect confidence and trust in His Father during His severe conflict with the powerful foe. Jesus, in the victory which he gained here, has left us a perfect example, showing us that our only safety is in the firm trust and unwavering confidence in God. Christ refused to presume upon the mercy of His Father by not allowing himself to be put in peril. It would have been a presumptuous act that would have made it necessary for His Heavenly Father to display His power to save Him from danger.

The Elmer Gantry Syndrome

Elmer Gantry is a fictional character in the novel of the same name written by Sinclair Lewis in 1926. The novel is a satirical characterization of a young, narcissistic, womanizing college athlete who abandons his early ambition to become a lawyer. The legal profession does not suit the unethical Gantry. After college, he attends a Baptist seminary, and he is ordained as a Baptist minister. While managing to hide certain sexual indiscretions, he is thrown out of the seminary before completing his bachelor of divinity because he is too drunk to attend a church where he is supposed to preach. Especially ironic is the way he champions love, an emotion of which he seems incapable. In his sermons, he preaches against ambition when he is so patently ambitious and organizes crusades against (mainly sexual) immorality when he has difficulty resisting sexual temptations.

After several years as a traveling salesman of farm equipment, he becomes a confidante of Sharon Falconer, a popular motivational speaker and evangelist with a "road church" show. Gantry becomes her lover but loses both her and his position when she and scores of attendants are killed in a tragic fire in her tent tabernacle. After this catastrophe, he briefly acts as a "New Thought" evangelist and eventually becomes a Methodist minister. He marries a local parishioner purely for the sake of appearances. Years later the Methodist leadership awards him a larger congregation in Lewis's fictional city of Zenith.

With his power and career in full tilt, Gantry manipulates local, state and national politics, which involves police raids against bootleggers and bar patrons. His corruption and power hunger contribute to the downfall, physical injury, and even death of key people around him. Lewis states at the beginning of Elmer Gantry that "no character in this book is the portrait of any actual person,"[1] but the reader is left in no doubt that Lewis's interpretation of his contemporary preachers - Billy Sunday (1862–1935) and Aimee Semple McPherson (1890–1944), influenced the spirit of the novel.

When the novel was published in 1927, some called it anti-Christian since Gantry used the pulpit to chase money and women. But Lewis wasn't actually critiquing all churches. With a bit of the same indignation as the biblical prophets, he sought to expose fraudsters who prey on others. In many ways, Lewis predicted preachers like Jim Bakker, the televangelist who went to prison in 1989 after having an affair and cheating people out of money.

Too many religious leaders in North America have fallen over the past 30 years. It has become so prevalent that we are no longer shocked when we hear the news that another preacher or televangelist has been removed temporarily or permanently from his or her ministry due to a moral failure. Some choose the path of rehabilitation and are able to return to their ministry, while others may not have a choice because not only did they fail morally, but they might have broken the law and had to be incarcerated.

It is ironic that most of the time, those who have experienced moral failings are those who formerly espoused righteousness and holy living – those who condemned certain moral sins – only to end up committing those same sins. The Bible loves a good redemption story, but forgiveness only goes so far. These religious leaders who fell from grace shocked the world when their crimes and scandals became public. The fallen pastors and leaders include some very famous men, some who preached against homosexuality and were themselves caught being gay. Others were found in adulterous relationships or sentenced to prison for pedophilia.

The pastors who have fallen into sin have all kinds of excuses: "it wasn't technically illegal, it was a youthful mistake, it was a conspiracy orchestrated by a certain group." But none of that excuses the hypocrisy of religious "authorities" preaching one standard for their flock and then flaunting those rules in their private lives. Presumptuous sin cuts in many ways. You can presume on the goodness of God and turn His grace into licentiousness – assuming the mercy He gave yesterday is what He'll give today (Jude 4). Or you can presume and turn God's grace into legalism – assuming the works you do today will satisfy God's holiness tomorrow (Matt. 7:22-23). Both seek to test the Lord, the former His goodness in order to sin, the latter His righteousness in order to boast.

Presumptuousness has two characteristics when compared to faith: First, presumption starts with an assumption; faith starts with a promise. Those who sit on a premise instead of standing on a promise are standing on slippery ground. Faith says God will "give us this day our daily bread"; unbelief says He won't; doubt says He might; but presumption believes the bread must be hot and buttered. It might be, but God's under no obligation. Abraham could sacrifice Isaac because God said in "Isaac," your seed shall come – a specific name attached to the promise (Heb. 11:17-19).

Second, presumption seeks to manipulate the outcome; faith waits patiently on the Lord (Hebrews. 6:15). Whether it's Hagar being given to Abraham to bring about the promised seed, Rebekah deceiving her husband Isaac to fulfill Jacob's destiny, or Moses murdering an Egyptian to help free his brethren, manipulation never advanced God's promises, only hindered them. Faith knows that God's will, done God's way, will never lack for God's supply and blessing. Therefore, don't presume on God. It's fatal. If faith is the assurance of things hoped for, then presumption is the controlling of things wished for, assuming that our position in God gives us entitlement.

The spirit of Elmer Gantry isn't a new phenomenon. We see some very remarkable acts of presumptuousness happening in the Early Church era. Through his servant John the Apostle, Jesus sent messages to the churches in Asia Minor. In some of these letters, we can see the church today as it struggles with some of the same things that they struggled with. Namely, lukewarmness, sexual immorality, affluence peddling, presumptuousness, comfort and spiritual deadness.

Although the seven letters in Revelation are tailored to the named churches, these churches and their stated deficiencies can symbolize all churches in one respect or another. Therefore, the instruction given to Revelation's congregations is relevant and valuable to Christian congregations today. Particularly, we see the church in Laodicea, the apostate church, representing the current stage of church history.

The letters to these seven churches remind us that Christianity can never be just a doctrine that we believe in, but it must also be a lifestyle that we consistently practice. Christ is concerned about our morals, our values, our priorities, our entertainment — everything about how we use our talents and spend our time. But the subtle (and sometimes not-so-subtle) influences of our world sometimes cause us to lower our standards and put less emphasis on holiness and purity. And often, we don't even notice the change.

The Church in Pergamum

A few of the Seven Churches in the Revelation were doing quite well. But the Church in Pergamum, which was experiencing the world coming to them, was feeling the power of their pagan idolatry and the acts of immorality that went with that. Needless to say, a lot of compromises were taking place, resulting in confusion and strange doctrines. Hence, Jesus' message to them:

> I know where you live—where Satan has his throne. Yet you remain true to my name. You did not renounce your faith in me, not even in the days of Antipas, my faithful witness, who was put to death in your city— where Satan lives. Nevertheless, I have a few things against you: There are some among you who hold to the teaching of Balaam, who taught Balak to entice the Israelites to sin so that they ate food sacrificed to idols and committed sexual immorality. Likewise, you

also have those who hold to the teaching of the Nicolaitans (Revelation 2:13-15).

What Jesus said to the Church in Pergamum, he says to us as well today.

"Repent therefore! Otherwise, I will soon come to you and will fight against them with the sword of my mouth" (Revelation 2:16).

The Church in Thyatira

Thyatira was a wealthy commercial city. Jesus' letter to the church in Thyatira praises it for growing in faith and service. However, the church's downfall was its devotion to a false prophet, which led some members to commit idolatry and sexual immorality. Although the false prophet remained unrepentant, Jesus affirms that the congregation can still repent by turning away from the prophet's ways.

> Nevertheless, I have this against you: You tolerate that woman Jezebel, who calls herself a prophet. By her teaching, she misleads my servants into sexual immorality and the eating of food sacrificed to idols. I have given her time to repent of her immorality, but she is unwilling. So I will cast her on a bed of suffering, and I will make those who commit adultery with her suffer intensely unless they repent of

her ways. I will strike her children dead. Then all the churches will know that I am he who searches hearts and minds, and I will repay each of you according to your deeds (Revelation 2:20-23).

The Church in Laodicea

Laodicea was a prosperous industrial and commercial center. Jesus' letter to the church in Laodicea wastes no time denouncing the congregation for its lukewarm faith, threatening to "spit" the congregation out of His mouth. Christ scolds this church for allowing its economic prosperity to cause its spiritual bankruptcy and reveals that, despite its economic wealth, they were *wretched, pitiful, poor, blind and naked.* And the worst part is; *they did nor realize it.* Like Samson, they were presuming on the grace and favour of God, taking him for granted. Like Samson, they did not realize that they were 'running on empty.' Jesus wanted them to know that only He could provide spiritual wealth. Those in Laodicea's church, as well as us today, who open the door to Christ, will share in His heavenly banquet and have the right to sit with Him on His throne. Jesus said to them;

You say, 'I am rich; I have acquired wealth and do not need a thing.' *But you do not realize* that you are wretched, pitiful, poor, blind and naked. I counsel you to buy from me gold refined in the fire, so you can become rich; and white clothes to wear, so you can cover your shameful nakedness; and salve to put on your eyes, so you can see. Those whom I love, I rebuke and discipline. So be earnest and repent. Here I am! I stand at the door and knock. If anyone hears my voice and opens the door, I will come in and eat with that person, and they with me (Revelation 3:17-20).

Like the church of Laodicea and the others that felt a sense of entitlement, it's easy to become complacent in our faith during times of abundance. Christ warns us in this passage that he will "spit out" lukewarm disciples. Instead, He urges us to keep seeking the Lord's face even after His hand has bestowed riches in our lives. We must not lose sight of the fact that all these letters were written to the Church! The question for us is this: Are we open to being confronted with our sin? Are we willing to change, to allow the Lord to mold, shape and correct us as needed? Are we willing to confess our sins and admit our errors? Our willingness to repent is absolutely essential if we are to be the Lord's people.

Christ is Concerned About Our Lifestyle

I wonder if being comfortable and complacent isn't the besetting sin of the Twenty-First Century church – among some of us who call ourselves Followers of Jesus! I wonder if we have, unconsciously, lazily, selfishly, formally grown into a discipleship that Jesus himself would not acknowledge? Is our definition of being a Christian simply to enjoy the privileges of worship, be generous at no expense to ourselves, have a good, easy time surrounded by pleasant friends and comfortable things, live respectably, and, in the end, have a nice funeral? According to the word of God, there is a lot more to true discipleship.

Jesus, in so many ways and on so many occasions, has preached self-denial. We must all be willing to deny ourselves and take up the cross in order to follow Christ! We must keep reminding ourselves that we have not been called to a life of ease but to a life of sacrifice. How much is the Christianity of our day suffering for Christ? Our lack of self-denial results in presumptuousness, ease, comfort, luxury, and elegance of living! Jesus Christ is concerned about our lifestyle. He's concerned not just with how we behave when we're in the church building but with how we behave from day to day, in our homes, at work, driving around town, standing in line at the grocery store. Christ is concerned about our lifestyle!

Ultimately, God works in all things – including tragedies of leadership – for the good of those who love Him. When a disaster happens, God is not done but is working it for good. Joseph's immoral brothers failed miserably, but God was working it together for Joseph's good, the brothers' good, the nation's good, and for the good of you and me. When Peter failed and denied Christ, God was not finished but was using the failure to strengthen all Christians everywhere. God wastes nothing. It's one thing to mourn the failure of a leader. It's another thing to join God in turning that mourning into proactive steps to produce something good.

Chapter 9

Avoiding the Lure of Sex, Money and Power

There are three temptations that are prevalent in our world today, but they are not new. Even in the days of Samson – the days of the Judges they had firmly established themselves in their society. These three temptations have been responsible for the struggles of many of God's followers. They are *sex, money*, and *power*. The damage done when a person gives in to temptation is often severe, as we have seen in the lives of so many of God's servants.

For example, when King David committed adultery he was forgiven by God. Yet, David also lost all moral authority in his home and in the nation. This was a very costly sin! And when he used his political power to have Uriah the Hittite murdered, the cost of this sin was the loss of his own son (2 Samuel 12:14). Regarding the failings and punishment of the Israelites in the Old Testament, including Samson, Paul says; *"These things happened to them as examples and were written down as warnings for us on whom the culmination of the ages has come. So, if you think you are standing firm, be careful that you don't fall!"* (1 Corinthians 10:11-12).

This is great advice from Paul. He alerts us to the possibility of falling, even when we believe we are standing on secure ground. This alertness includes thinking about what's at stake. As we ponder the life of Samson, we cannot truly say that he counted the cost of his actions. He allowed his carnal desires to overcome the call that God had on his life. He played with the Holy Spirit's presence until he became so desensitized by continual actions of disobedience that he was totally unaware that the Lord had left him.

Avoiding the Lure of Sex

The War Within

> One man wrote this anonymously because he was embarrassed. Embarrassed for his wife and children, yes, but embarrassed most for himself. He tells of his personal battle with lust but adds that if he believed he were the only one who fought in that war, he would not waste emotional energy drudging up stained and painful memories. But he believes his experience is not uncommon, if not typical of pastors, writers and conference speakers. He goes on to say no one talks about it, no one writes about it. But it is there, like an acknowledged cancer, that metastasizes best when no one goes for x-rays or examines themselves for lumps.[2]

The war within exposes a process of indulgence, of people following their sexual desires wherever they may lead. Our society seems strangely schizophrenic on the wisdom of such an approach. On the one hand, authors advocating a so-called 'new celibacy' appear on talk shows, and write magazine articles on the ethic of intimacy. On the other hand, one needs only to flip through the advertisements in other magazines and on social media to realize our society's approving attitude toward lust.

Pornography radically disconnects sex from its intended purpose. Human sexuality, a gift from God, was designed to express a relationship between a man and a woman in the context of marriage, but pornography separates out one aspect of that gift – a physical appeal – and focuses on it. In the "Hart Report," Dr. Archibald D. Hart writes in regard to pornographic magazines. He says;

> "They catch just about every young boy's eyes sooner or later. High-gloss, colorful and titillating. They line the magazine racks at every corner newsstand. Some women may take a peek inside, but mostly, they appeal to men – even very young men-in-the-making. Some say it's a right of passage for teenagers to grow up with them. But the power of, the sexual images presented in pornography is so powerful that it always leaves a lasting impression. If it didn't, no one would make a profit. Magazine vendors would switch to selling real estate." [3]

When we think of sexual misdeeds involving local church ministers, events of recent years force us to think of the following names: Jim Bakker, and Jimmy Swaggart and others. Yet, it's an unfair association. I believe high-profile televangelists and local church leaders have very little in common. The intentional, wilful sexual escapades of the rich and famous are not the usual stuff of local church ministry.

For most of us, sexual temptation is the unconscious background static of everyday living, not the stereophonic soap opera of hotel trysts and red-light liaisons. In its own way, local church temptation is every bit as powerful and dangerous. But the dynamics are different. Still, the association is there. And to mention that we are tempted sexually by anyone, whether wife, counsellor, mentor, friend or colleague – is to throw oneself into the unsavoury company in most minds. So where can a sympathetic or, better yet, helpful ear be found?

When Samson, in the midst of God's call in his life, got involved in sexual escapades with Philistine women, it wasn't unconscious background static of everyday living. They were intentional, well-thought-out acts done with the full knowledge that he was being disobedient to the word and will of God. He was well aware of his call to deliver God's people from the tyranny of the Philistines; but instead, he purposefully had encounters with them that left him weak and devoid of the Holy Spirit in his life. That's what disobedience does. In Samson's case, it led to a downward spiral that ended in death.

For the Christ Follower, however, the reputation of Christ and his church is impacted. Throughout the New Testament you can read of Paul's concern for the reputation of the church. Why? Simply for the sake of the people in the church? No. It's because Jesus' name is linked to the reputation of the church. When you think about it, it's stunning to realize that Jesus would allow this connection to exist – that his name be linked to the reputation of the church, but he does! When such unwholesome escapades take place in the church, the credibility of the church's teaching of what's right and wrong will be diminished.

The apostle Paul explains this well in Romans 2:1; *You, therefore, have no excuse, you who pass judgment on someone else, for at whatever point you judge the other, you are condemning yourself, because you who pass judgment do the same things* (Romans 2:1). It's already very difficult for the church or individual believers to represent truth to the culture, regarding evils such as abortion on demand and others; This difficulty is magnified when many Christians are involved in their own sins such as pornography, lying, greed, and taking advantage of others.

The Psychology of Samson

It's inevitable that the record of Samson in Gaza and the Valley of Sorek would prompt some to reflect upon the psychology of Samson as a womanizer. They may ask questions like, "Why are some men womanizers?" "Why was Samson a womanizer?" Some experts have summarized the psychological basis for Samson's womanizing like this: They say some men are womanizers, and what is wrong with them is that they have issues with commitment and intimacy that they refuse to deal with and escape into a fantasy relationship with another woman time after time. Other men, though, are seeking something they feel is missing in their primary relationship – such as understanding, excitement, or a woman that is challenging to them.

Others say most womanizers are simply very lonely men who usually have or often claim to have a high sex drive and a lust for sexual variety. It has been postulated that such men often don't like women or even sex. Some womanizers, it is believed, have a disease or an addiction in which they see women as the enemy. They think of "being a real man" as escaping a woman's control and as being someone who can powerfully manipulate and deceive women. They believe that, like a rapist, the womanizer seeks power and superiority. How does all this apply to Samson?

If when Samson encountered Delilah, he had been all rippling muscles, Delilah would not have had to ask where his strength lay. His strength was from God, not from his muscles. And yet he would've been perceived as a "real man", a strong man. It was just enigmatic to everyone how this was when an ordinary man acted so strong. And so, perhaps Samson acted up to the level of how others perceived him.

He indulged the 'woman thing' because that's what heroic 'strong men' of his time were supposed to do. He felt he had to act *as if* he had a strong libido when perhaps he didn't. And, of course, he was lonely... the picture of the young man wandering off from his parents when they were on their way down to talk with his first wife... meeting a lion... here's the very cameo of a lonely man.

Also, his special calling from God would've made him lonely. This would have led to his problem with intimacy with others in an Israel of cowards and semi-spirituality. He wasn't much understood by anyone... David had Jonathan, Gideon had Phurah, Moses had Aaron, and Joshua had Caleb, but Samson apparently had nobody at all. His whole behavior with women, Delilah especially but actually all the recorded women in his life, speaks of a man who relished 'escaping' a woman's control and being someone who can powerfully manipulate and deceive women. But this is all speculation. The bottom line is that Samson sinned.

Reflecting on Samson, we get a glimpse of why he could have been a lonely man. But most leaders are lonely and not understood by our world or even our own community. We, too, try to act up to the expectations and images that others place upon us, but this doesn't justify us! This is the lesson of Samson. Sin is sin, even if our own faith and spiritual commitment have placed us in a situation where the loneliness and lack of being understood of itself create a psychological situation that leads to temptation. Falling to that temptation, even if, like Samson in Gaza, we preserve our faith and commitment in our deepest heart, and we usually pay the price for it.

Guarding Against Sexual Sin

Loneliness in ministry is a real thing. Sometimes, people hold us in such high esteem that we find ourselves without any friends. At other times, the reason for our loneliness could be brought about because of our attitude toward others. So, of course, having accountability in relationships is a wonderful thing! Have someone in your life with whom to discuss issues that may be affecting you on a personal level or in your ministry – a close friend, a mentor, or a discipleship group. But how can one stay clear of sin in the first place?

First, we have to recognize that there's a desire within all of us that will tempt us to stray from God's ways (see Romans 7). This desire is called "the flesh" in the New Testament. *Second*, we all need to remember that there's an enemy who is seeking our downfall by appealing to the desires of our flesh. *Third*, we'll need to seek out practical steps, even rules for our lives, that can close the door to sin. This shouldn't be considered legalism. It's being realistic and finding the necessary tools that will help us to live an overcoming life. At times, you'll hear people discourage practical steps by calling them "legalistic." But those who have intentionally attempted to grow in godly character come to see just how formidable the sinful nature and the enemy really are.

With this heightened awareness, a follower of Jesus who wants to grow understands that the best strategy for avoiding these temptations is to keep himself/herself out of their path (i.e. avoiding any triggers or places of opportunity)! That is, putting practical steps in place that reflect the fact that we do love Jesus and are responding to what he's already done for us. Even Jesus pointed to dealing with sexual sin very intentionally. Matthew 5:29-30; *"If your right eye causes you to sin, gouge it out and throw it away. It is better for you to lose one part of your body than for your whole body to be thrown into hell. And if your right-hand causes you to sin, cut it off and throw it away. It is better for you to lose one part of your body than for your whole body to go into hell."*

Obviously, Jesus was using hyperbole in his challenge. Most would still sin with their mind, even if they had no hands! However, Jesus did take the consequences of sexual sin so seriously that he endorsed whatever it would take to steer clear of it. We should purpose in our hearts to do whatever is necessary to live a life of sexual purity. Proverbs calls this approach discretion or wisdom. The person who develops such traits will experience much less pain in life! Consider these words carefully;

It will save you from the unfaithful wife who tries to lead you into adultery with pleasing words. She leaves the husband she married when she was young. She ignores the promise she made before God. Her house is on the way to death; those who took that path are now all dead (Proverbs 2:16-18).

Another passage in Proverbs says; *Now then, my sons, listen to me; do not turn aside from what I say. Keep to a path far from her [adulterous woman], do not go near the door of her house.* This is a practical step, or might it be said, "take a step by staying away from her steps!" (Proverbs 5:7-11)

The Pursuit of Pleasure

It is quite ironic that Solomon wrote most of these 'Proverbs' concerning how we are to live when his life was just the opposite. He pursued a life of pleasure and materialism, even though he started with such a humble attitude. When he became king, and God enquired of him what is the desire of his heart;

Solomon answered, "You have shown great kindness to your servant, my father David because he was faithful to you, righteous, and upright in heart. You have continued this great kindness to him and have given him a son to sit on his throne this very day. "Now, O LORD my God, you have made your servant king in place of my father David. But I am only a little child and do not know how to carry out my duties. Your servant is here among the people you have chosen, a great people, too numerous to count or number. So give your servant a discerning heart to govern your people and to distinguish between right and wrong. For who is able to govern this great people of yours?" The Lord was pleased that Solomon had asked for this. (1 Kings 3:6-10)

So, where did Solomon go wrong? Without a doubt, I think his biggest problem was giving himself over to the pursuit of pleasure. In Ecclesiastes 2 there is a description in Solomon's own words, where he's talking about his pursuit of pleasure. He describes planting vineyards, gardens, and orchards. Acquiring male and female servants and great numbers of herds and flocks. And for entertainment, acquiring male and female singers and musical instruments (Ecclesiastes 2:4-9). It just goes on and on talking about all this stuff, and at the end, he literally confesses, "Whatever my eyes desired, I did not keep from them. I did not withhold my heart from any pleasure."

As if that weren't bad enough, on top of all that, it appears that sexual pleasure really dominated Solomon's life, leading him to accumulate 700 wives and 300 concubines. This pursuit of pleasure didn't just distract Solomon like his pursuit of wealth did, Solomon's pursuit of pleasure led him completely astray. That is one of the things that the pursuit of pleasure will do for any of us, even today.

I think there are at least three things we really have to be aware of when it comes to pursuing pleasure. When it boils down to it, pleasure is a feeling, and when we make the pursuit of a feeling one of the chief aims in our life, we've automatically elevated feelings into a dominant role in our life. Another thing pursuing pleasure does is keep the inward flow of our life focused on getting instead of giving. This is the very opposite of the way Jesus taught us to live. The third thing is that pleasure keeps our affection set on the things of this world. We're very focused on what we are possessing, accumulating, and experiencing here in this world. We simply cannot resist the pull of the world when pleasure and experiencing pleasure are so important to us.

When we look at Solomon's life, we see a man who started his reign by consecrating the Temple of the Lord. But in the end, he becomes a shameless idolater because he doesn't restrain his pursuit of pleasure. That kind of disobedience is inevitable for someone who idolizes pleasure. If we exalt pleasure more than godliness like Solomon, all of us will soon be willing to disobey even the clearest commands of the Lord in exchange for pleasure.

Finding God's Design

As humans, we bear the image of the Divine. We are made "after the likeness" of God, who by nature of existing as three persons bonded together in eternal oneness (Trinity), created relational counterparts, male and female, to bear his image (Genesis. 1:26). Genesis 1:27 states, *"So God created mankind in his own image, in the image of God he created them; male and female he created them."* The Bible continues, *"That is why a man leaves his father and mother and is united to his wife, and they become one flesh"* (Genesis 2:24). This verse sets forth the biblical pattern for marriage as instituted by God in the beginning: one man is united to one woman in matrimony, and the two form one new family. Jesus confirms all of this in Matthew 19:3-6, pointing toward marriage as a male/female, one-flesh union from the beginning:

> Some Pharisees came to him (Jesus) to test him. They asked, "Is it lawful for a man to divorce his wife for any and every reason?" "Haven't you read," he replied, "that at the beginning the Creator 'made them male and female,' and said, 'For this reason a man will leave his father and mother and be united to his wife, and the two will become one flesh'? So they are no longer two, but one flesh. Therefore, what God has joined together, let no one separate" (Matthew 19:3-6).

Marriage is used throughout the Bible as a reflection of Christ's relationship to the Church itself (Ephesians 5:32). Just as adoption points us to a deeper understanding of all believers being adopted into God's family through Christ, biblical marriage and families point us to a deeper understanding of the Church as the bride of Christ.

> "When the Creator devised the one-flesh relationship, He placed within it the potential for a sexual intimacy that could bless marriages almost beyond belief. This potential has not always been understood, but today therapists and researchers are discovering that genuine sexual intimacy has a remarkable power to heal, renew, refresh, restore, and sustain the marriage relationship." [4]

As a pastor for seventeen years, I have observed that marriage, with its tremendous significance, often turns out to be the least-prepared-for event of life. Even as divorce takes on epidemic proportions, young couples continue to venture into marriage remarkably unprepared. Sometimes, there is a brief meeting with the minister before the wedding, then an often elaborate ceremony. Soon afterward, the newlyweds are on their own, to hit or miss in their quest for happiness, while family and friends hope for the best. So, premarital counselling must be an essential part of the preparation. It is not only a preventive measure, protecting against family breakups, but it also can trigger a positive course of action, which will bring pleasure and joy to the marriage.

Avoiding the Lure of Money

Throughout the Scriptures, the love of money has always been an issue that has caused many people to do regrettable things. Beginning with Joseph's brothers who sold him into slavery for twenty shekels of silver, *Judah said to his brothers, "What will we gain if we kill our brother and cover up his blood? Come, let's sell him to the Ishmaelites and not lay our hands on him; after all, he is our brother, our own flesh and blood." His brothers agreed. So when the Midianite merchants came by, his brothers pulled Joseph up out of the cistern and sold him for twenty shekels (about eight ounces) of silver to the Ishmaelites, who took him to Egypt* (Genesis 37:26-38).

Judas Iscariot's name became so synonymous with betrayal that he is hardly mentioned in the Gospels without a phrase such as "who betrayed him" or "who became a traitor." We aren't sure exactly what motivated him to betray Jesus, except we do know he struggled with greed, and he agreed to betray Jesus to the authorities who wanted Jesus dead for a price—thirty pieces of silver. He arranged to lead them to Jesus and give them a signal. He would let them know which one was Jesus by greeting him with a kiss. Thus, "Judas's kiss" has become the quintessential metaphor for betrayal.

Jesus' question in reply says it all: "*Judas, are you betraying the Son of Man with a kiss?*" (Luke 22:48).

Then there was Ananias, who, together with his wife Sapphira, lied about the money they had received from the sale of a piece of property. They held back a portion of the money and lied to the apostles that what they had donated was the full price. Then Peter said, "*Ananias, how is it that Satan has so filled your heart that you have lied to the Holy Spirit and have kept for yourself some of the money you received for the land? Didn't it belong to you before it was sold? And after it was sold, wasn't the money at your disposal? What made you think of doing such a thing? You have not lied just to human beings but to God*" (Acts 5:3-4).

And finally, there was Delilah, who betrayed Samson for a large sum of money! *Sometime later, he (Samson) fell in love with a woman in the Valley of Sorek whose name was Delilah. The rulers of the Philistines went to her and said, "See if you can lure him into showing you the secret of his great strength and how we can overpower him so we may tie him up and subdue him. Each one of us will give you eleven hundred shekels of silver*" (Judges 16:4-5). Blinded by the promise of a great sum of money in the form of silver, Delilah went to work on Samson, wearing him down until he truthfully disclosed the secret of his great strength. After putting him to sleep on her lap, she called for someone to shave off the seven braids of his hair and so began to subdue him. And his strength left him." We shouldn't be surprised if a relationship built on self-interest and mistrust is consummated by betrayal.

Betrayal! We have probably all experienced it at one time or another. But betrayal for money is quite another thing. Nevertheless, we shouldn't be surprised if and when it happens. It's the cruelest form of traitorous behavior, as it not only puts a price on your head, it stabs you in the back only after inviting the embrace. Its victims didn't see it coming, and that's why its pain cuts the deepest and lasts the longest. As in the case of Samson and Delilah, what might have begun to grow as a truly genuine relationship on Samson's part ended with Samson being shorn, bound, and blinded as his downward spiral continued.

We must avoid the lure of money at all costs by viewing the money we have and the ability to produce wealth as from God? Let's consider carefully what God says to his people; *You may say to yourself, "My power and the strength of my hands have produced this wealth for me." But remember the LORD your God, for it is he who gives you the ability to produce wealth, and so confirms his covenant, which he swore to your ancestors, as it is today* (Deuteronomy 8:17-18). Therefore, we must realize that everything we have is from God! And we're responsible to be wise with what we have been given.

Guarding Against the Lure and Abuse of Power

When we talk about power, some people may want to exclude themselves, thinking that they do not have any power. But did you know we all have power? Whether one is the President of a company, the CEO, a Pastor, or a regular employee, we all have power! Of course, the word "power" is sometimes seen negatively because it's often used improperly or abused. What is meant by "power" is influence. We must consider these very important questions – do we use our power or influence to build others up and further the kingdom of God? Or do we misuse or waste our power or influence? Do we use our power to abuse those over whom we have the authority, or do we seek to bring justice to those who are being oppressed?

The abuse of power is ancient. It goes all the way back to the Garden of Eden, where Cain killed his brother Abel. As brothers, they had an influence on each other's lives. Cain severely misused his influence. Whatever his motive was – maybe jealousy – he abused the relationship. Abuse of power or influence can take many forms, including more subtle ways than murder! Again, it's a stewardship question to be considered in light of Jeremiah's words, *"Lord, I know that people's lives are not their own; it is not for them to direct their steps"* (Jeremiah 10:23).

You might have influence wherever you are. People may report to you at work. You may volunteer at church or the community, where others either look up to you or give you influence in your life. You may be a parent. You may be a child of elderly parents. (as people get frailer, they often give much influence to their children). You may be in a close relationship with a spouse, friends, or within a small group. Even when relationships are "equal," we still have influence. So, we must realize that we are accountable to God in whatever we do and act with love and grace.

One of King David's loyal soldiers – called David's "mighty men" – was Uriah the Hittite. When Uriah was off at battle, David slept with Uriah's wife, Bathsheba. When she became pregnant, David had Uriah called back from the battle to go home and be with his wife to make the pregnancy look like his. Uriah refused to return to his house out of loyalty to his fellow soldiers because they were roughing it on the battlefield. So, David went with Plan B, returning Uriah to the battlefield and secretly telling the commander to withdraw troops from Uriah in the heat of the battle so that he would be killed.

Plan B came with subpoints, such as the lecture David would give when he learned that the soldiers had made such a foolish move on the battlefield. Plan B worked, and David could have Uriah's widow as often as he wanted without suspicion. David used his power and influence to commit not only adultery and murder but he also used his power to blame the soldiers for making a move, which he himself had orchestrated. One of the best ways to check our lives for any type of sin due to the abuse of power is to reflect on the word of God as we seek to follow the plan he has marked out for our lives.

We should not manipulate or seek control through harsh words, passive aggressiveness, lies, or by promising or withholding things or money from people. And we must seek to build others up by practicing the words of the Apostle Paul, "*Do nothing out of selfish ambition or vain conceit, but in humility consider others better than yourselves. Each of you should look not only to your own interests but also to the interests of others*" (Philippians 2:3-4). We must not use our influence to try to get what we want. We must trust God to supply what we need. Yes, we need support from others! But most of all, we need the help of the Lord. And finally, if we witness an abuse of power or influence, we must be willing to both pray and appropriately act?

It is fairly obvious that the triple threat of sex, money, and power or influence go together hand in hand. This is an example, one in which the powerful used their money and influence as someone in a position of trust to manipulate and abuse others. When such things happen, the victims usually blame themselves for allowing themselves to be influenced and manipulated by someone with whom they had placed their trust. The anger may be suppressed for a while but later manifests itself in many different ways.

It's been over three decades since the world found out about the 15 minutes she spent in a Florida hotel room with televangelist Jim Bakker. But Jessica Hahn says it's only been in the last two years that she's finally confronted her anger about what happened and how it's affected the rest of her life. She says she's angry at Bakker, founder of the onetime PTL empire near Charlotte, for using his power and his image as a man of God to manipulate her, then a 21-year-old church secretary, into having a sexual relationship. "He just believed that everybody should serve him because he was serving God," she said of Bakker. [5]

Televangelists Jim and Tammy Faye Bakker had built a multimillion-dollar empire in South Carolina. Known as PTL, it was a conglomerate of Christian-based businesses. In addition to a Christian broadcasting network, it included a theme park, water park, and residential complex. It raked in millions of dollars per year. Jim was known for his all-inclusive messages. Tammy Faye became famous for her garish makeup — false eyelashes, red rouge, and heavy lipstick. But everything came crashing down in 1987 when the *Charlotte Observer* began investigating the organization's finances. Among the newspaper's findings: was that Jim Bakker had paid $279,000 to Jessica Hahn, a church secretary. Soon, the story became more tawdry. Hahn alleged that she had been raped by Bakker in 1980 when she was 21. He acknowledged that he had once had sex with her but insisted that the sex was consensual. The financial mismanagement that was uncovered was enough to get authorities to notice. Bakker was found guilty of 24 counts of fraud and sentenced to 45 years in prison. He was paroled after about five years behind bars. [6]

At this juncture, it is good for us to remind ourselves of the Apostle Peter's admonition to not conform to the evil desires we once had before we were set free by the power of God through Jesus Christ. He writes;

"As obedient children, do not conform to the evil desires you had when you lived in ignorance. But just as he who called you is holy, so be holy in all you do" (1 Peter 1:14-15).

Chapter 10
When Leaders (Fail) Fall

How often have we turned on the news or opened up a social media account to be greeted by a headline about a prominent Christian leader who was engrossed in scandal. Our first thoughts are probably, "Not again." It seems like every few weeks, we learn about more prominent evangelical leaders who have moved from *rise* to *fall* due to toxic leadership, financial mismanagement, or moral failure. You may throw your hands in the air and ask, why does this keep happening?

Terry Muck, former editor of Leadership Journal, in his book; "Sins of the Body," relates this account regarding one of his friends who called him from across the country:

"Something terrible has happened." The tense voice was my friend's, calling from across the country. "Yesterday our pastor left his wife and ran off with another woman." I was sad, but not shocked or even surprised. Fifteen years ago, I would have been shocked. Ten years ago, I would have been surprised. But I've heard the same story too many times now ever to be surprised again.

I recently spoke on sexual purity at a Bible college. During that week, many students came for counselling, including three I'll call Rachel, Barb, and Pam. Rachel got right to the point: "My parents sent me to one of my pastors for counselling, and I ended up sleeping with him." Later the same day, Barb, a church leader's daughter, told me through tears, "My dad has had sex with me for years, and now he's starting on my sisters." The next evening, I met with Pam. Her story? "I came to Bible college to get away from an affair with my pastor."

For every well-known Christian television personality or author whose impropriety is widely publicized, there are any number of lesser known pastors, Bible teachers, and para-church workers who quietly resign or are fired for sexual immorality.[7]

The news seems to be filled on a regular basis, with yet another ministry leader or public figure being dismissed over issues such as abuse, addiction, anger issues, embezzlement, or sexual immorality —the list could go on. People who were esteemed as godly leaders, with followers numbering in the millions, are discovered to be broken, flawed, and even wicked. This situation is disheartening, and when that leader is someone we respect, news of their "behind-the-curtain" life can be particularly hard to take and may even derail us.

Over the last few years, news about leaders like Bill Hybels, Ravi Zacharias, and, most recently, Brian Houston of Hillsong Church have deeply impacted many of their followers on several levels. This leaves all of us wondering—what are we to do in situations like these? How should we respond when a Christian leader, especially a leader we respected, falls from grace?

Furthermore, ministry brings with it several built-in hazards – moral land mines – that can destroy us, our families, and our churches. Among them are our position of influence and that strange blend of ego-feeding flattery and debilitating criticism, which can fill us with either pride or despair. As a result, our perspective can be warped, and our resistance to temptation diminished. In addition, some of the endless tasks with which leaders are often faced, and the resulting disorienting fatigue, can make one oblivious to what's happening around them.

For some, the pendulum swings to the opposite side, and they clamor for a world without leaders, or at a minimum, any celebrity-type leaders. But even if every large church disbanded, and every Christian met in a small house church, someone would figure out how to do it really well, would write or podcast about it, millions would listen or follow, and we would be right back where we started with "celebrity-like leaders."

When no leader is appointed, typically, the loudest or most forceful voice in the room will become the de facto leader. Throughout Scripture, God used leaders to accomplish His purposes—Moses, Samson, David, Deborah, and Paul, to name a few. Most were flawed and exhibited human frailties, but they all had significant roles and have impacted tens of thousands. Leadership is a biblical concept. The problem is that we don't have enough biblical leaders. Sadly, this pandemic of leadership failure appears to be far from over.

Slide or Staircase

Stepping into leadership means stepping into mistakes, regrets, and many small but stinging failures. And if we are to survive in leadership, it will mean stepping *upward* on those mistakes — owning them, learning from them, and having the stability in Christ to keep leading after them. To some extent, of course, every fallen human is familiar with failure. Mistakes follow us from the womb; we learn regret at a very early age – like learning the alphabet. However, for at least two reasons, leadership has a special way of drawing failure to the surface.

First, leadership provides a public platform for the kinds of mistakes we are already making. Surely Moses made blunders while building a family in Midian, David while shepherding his father's flocks, and Peter while fishing the Sea of Galilee. But their mistakes were more or less private — pebbles tossed into the pond, their ripples small and few. But then Moses began building a nation, David began shepherding a kingdom, and Peter began fishing for people. And all of a sudden, their private failures became public and subject to greater scrutiny.

Second, leadership affords many more opportunities for failure than we had before. Among the family, among the sheep, and among the fish, opportunities for failure were present but more limited. When leadership called Moses and, David, and Peter out of those worlds, worlds where they felt some semblance of success and control, their chances of failure multiplied. Leadership, at its core, involves public initiative and risk-taking. Leaders try new ventures; they aim, by God's grace, to bring new realities into being; they call people to follow down paths not yet ventured. And sometimes, the efforts of even the best leaders fall apart, and the risks return to smack them in the face.

Two Different Ways to Go

A few failures and mistakes sting. A few dozen will cause deep wounds. And then, over time, as mistakes rise even higher, we may feel ourselves standing before a small mountain of regret. It may seem like a monument to our incompetence. At this point, leaders may choose two different ways to go.

The *first* temptation is to protect ourselves from the

vulnerability of leadership by wearing a cast-iron cloak. Criticism no longer reaches our skin. Failures no longer wound because we refuse to feel them. Slowly, the once-lowly son of Kish becomes proud King Saul, hard and high, spiritually desensitized, safe from the sting of failure — and safe from the grace of God.

The *second* and perhaps more common temptation is to run away. Ditch everything – follow Peter back to Galilee, back to the fishing boat, back to some private sphere where no one is watching and you know what you're doing (John 21:3). Go back to where your mistakes and failures are not so glaring and where the consequences are not very grave. Or alternatively, keep "leading," but stop trying so hard to please everyone. Nothing ventured, nothing lost.

"We can attempt no risks, and leave the mountain taking to others. Lead from the land of 'Safety'. But if every leader stung by failure stepped away, the church would have no leaders." [8]

Now, stepping away from leadership is not always a bad thing. Maybe, in the wake of some particularly jarring failure — or after a longer pattern of missteps — we really do need to step back for a season and find our identity again in unhurried communion with Christ. Maybe we'll start leading again after a time. Or maybe, through much prayer and counsel, we'll decide not to return to formal leadership. And in some cases, that would be okay.

The body of Christ has many members, a handful of whom are leaders, all of whom are indispensable (1 Corinthians 12:22). Somehow, then, we need another way, a way of treating mistakes like so many steps, which over time, the Lord raises us into more faithful and fruitful leadership.

"We need grace to see not only how leaders make mistakes but how mistakes can make leaders. With God's help, we can allow the mistakes to shape us and mold us into the tools and vessels that God requires us to become." [9]

A Failure Can Be Stepping Stones

In his kindness, God filled his Scriptures with stories of leaders who failed but didn't finish there, who crashed but didn't burn. Yes, we read here of men like Saul and Judas and Demas, leaders whose failures took them to that downward spiral that leads to death. But we also read of men like Moses and David, Peter and the other disciples, whose maturity as leaders progressed on a step-by-step upward climb. We may find help from Peter in particular. His failure may have been a bigger failure than the kind we have been considering, but his story still gives us context for how we might step upward on our own failures, however large or small.

Own Your Failure

That morning, after Peter denied it, Jesus revealed more of Peter than Peter had ever seen. Just the night before, he swore he would die before he denied Jesus; then one, two, three: "I do not know him" (Luke 22:57). The rooster crowed, Jesus looked at Peter, and in that one brief moment, he saw himself for who he was. Instead of fleeing from such agonizing knowledge, though, he owned it. First, "he went out and wept bitterly" (Luke 22:60). Then he returned to his friends (Luke 24:10-12). And then, finally, on that early-morning Galilean shore, he offered no rationalization, no justification, no excuse (John 21:1-17). Failure had owned Peter on Good Friday — and here, standing before his gracious Lord, Peter owns his failure.

Sometimes, of course, we may fail because of weakness rather than of sin. Sometimes, failure does not reveal our guilt as much as our immaturity, ignorance, or incompetence in certain areas. Either way, the process still uncovers parts of us we need to see most desperately. Therefore, fully owning our failures is still the path of humility and wisdom. So, we should receive and embrace our failures. When others look around for someone responsible, let them see us taking ownership. The strength for such a painful embrace comes, in large part, from the confidence that failure lies well within God's sovereign promise to work it for our good.

Without failure, Peter would have remained self-confident and self-deceived; so would we. And so, in his sovereignty, Jesus sometimes allows his people to pass through the sift of failure (Luke 22:31-32). He does not, however, keep them there. If, like Peter, we feel the sting but refuse to run, we will find a future beyond failure. We also will find that failures teach a thousand lessons to those who are willing to pause, look them in the face, and learn from them.

Learn from Failures

Too often, we may allow the pain of the present moment to keep us from learning from failure. Today, the failure hurts. Today, we feel embarrassed. Today, we would rather soothe or distract ourselves than take our mistakes by the hand. We may forget that, in failure, God often has *tomorrow* in mind. Jesus tells Peter that he should strengthen his brothers when he has turned around. Jesus knew that when Peter turned again, repentant and then healed, he would be a different Peter. Outside that dark courtyard, self-confidence drained from Peter with his many bitter tears.

But on that Galilean shore, love for Jesus rose in Peter like a miraculous catch of fish. Failure today made Peter an apostle tomorrow — now so much stronger in Christ, now so much more wary of self. But only because he *learned* from failure. Sometimes, replaying our failures leads only to a fresh sense of shame or condemnation. But what if we returned to the scene not alone and exposed but alongside our forgiving Lord? And what if we asked him to help us review our failures with an eye toward tomorrow? We might find that errors become humility, mistakes become stepping stones, regrets become wisdom, self-inadequacy becomes Christ-sufficiency, and failures become reliable stairs.

Keep on Leading

Having owned our mistakes and learned what we can from them, we might imagine Jesus lifting us up from the ground, looking us in the eye, and offering both a question and a call. "Do you love me?" he asks Peter (John 21:15-17). Before the failure, Peter's love was real but shallow; now, as his risen Redeemer restores him, his love is real and deep. Amazingly, failure can do the same for us — taking the love *of* Jesus from theory to reality, taking our love *for* Jesus from shallow to deep.

The question also sets Peter and us on firmer ground. If leadership is mainly about *us* — our praise, our validation — then failures will either send us running away or wrapping that cast-iron shield around our hearts. But if leadership is ultimately about Jesus — his worship, his worth — then we can make ourselves vulnerable again for him. Yes, we have failed. Yes, we may fail again and feel again all the pain of falling on our faces. But we love him. And love can risk being broken.

Finally, having asked us the question, Jesus bids us to respond again to the call we heard so long ago: "Follow me" (John 21:19). Prepare your next sermon, plan the next meeting, schedule that counseling appointment, and chart the next course for your ministry. And by a miracle of grace, keep connected to the true vine so that you may bear abundant fruit.

Responding to Leaders' Failures

Don't Rejoice or Judge

When news surfaces of another leadership failure, the details coming out can be titillating, intriguing, and gossip-laden, we may find ourselves drawn in with curiosity about what happened in a hunger to learn all of the juicy details. If we're not careful, we can become like readers of a Christianized version of the National Enquirer. We may even find ourselves gloating about a leader we didn't particularly like. "I knew it all along" is an easy justification of our personal feelings of envy, jealousy, or dislike for a leader. While this is all too easy to fall into, none of this is healthy.

Instead, we need to remember that these are stories about real people with real families and real communities who are being deeply impacted—even torn apart—by this news. Many of these stories involve victims whose lives will never be the same. It is okay to find a reliable news source to determine the truth of what happened, but beyond that, we need to release the need to enter deeper into the gossip.

Like Job and his friends of the Old Testament, we ought to be willing to sit in silence together and grieve the losses—the loss of respect for Christians and churches in the media, the loss and the pain the leader, their family, and any victims will face, and the loss of direction for a community. When we grieve well, we give the Holy Spirit room to work in our own hearts and to lead us to pray for all those that have been hurt in some way.

Pray Earnestly

We may say we are praying for the situation, but I wonder, when these things occur, do we actually stop to pray? Do we read the stories, shake our heads in disbelief, and then simply move on? Or do we take time to wrestle with our own grief before the Lord and lift up the pain that the people connected to this story are experiencing? The Apostle Paul reminds us that we are together in the body of Christ:

But God has put the body together, giving greater honor to the parts that lacked it, so that there should be no division in the body, but that its parts should have equal concern for each other. If one part suffers, every part suffers with it; if one part is honored, every part rejoices with it (1 Corinthians 12:24-26)

When a leader falls, this could be a compelling reason to pause and pray—not only for the leader involved but for every pastor or leader we know. These stories seem to be pointing to some deeper, underlying issues of unhealthiness in the body of Christ. Rather than shaking our heads at these stories, what might happen if we collectively took hold of the burden for a healthy Church (the Body of Christ) and became people deeply committed to prayer? This, I believe, could lead to transformation in the future of the church and leadership.

It's the Giver, Not the Gift

One of the healthy gifts we may receive when a leader falls is the clear reminder that our faith is not meant to be in leaders themselves but in the God that they serve. We can become so enamored by someone's gifts that we forget Who gave them the gifts in the first place. We may be like the member of an audience who is so enraptured by the sound of a violin recital that we direct all of our affection to the violin itself. But in the end, the violin is only a tool, an instrument to be used in the capable hands of a master.

Regardless of how talented or gifted a Christian leader may be, those talents and gifts are from God. All Christian leaders are responsible for what God has given them, regardless of whether their talents and gifts can be considered exceptional or whether they are just mediocre—Leaders are only instruments, tools, or vessels to be used by the Master. Our faith should not be in the tool—the violin—but in our loving Master, who brings the tool to life and expresses His music to the world through the leader. If we find that our faith in a leader has been misplaced, we should not lose faith altogether. We should, instead, redirect our faith to the One who alone is faithful.

Leadership Encouragement

It is never too late to help a leader to make amends, and to support and redirect their lives. One of the questions that should be asked in any of these situations is; "Whether the leader had taken the right steps or whether others around them had provided enough help that would have enabled them to pursue their personal emotional, relational, and spiritual health?" Did they have a mentor? A group of peers where they could be rigorously honest? Did anyone give them space to deal with their own messiness? When someone becomes a leader, they may feel like they no longer have permission or the ability to be real.

Or, the leader might feel that the people they lead expect a level of perfection. In this warped view, the leader may feel an unspoken pressure to perform well and always look the part for fear that any failure or show of weakness would disqualify them from their position.

Yet, if we're honest, we all know that simply being given a position or a role doesn't do anything to automatically mature a person's character. We should absolutely vet leaders for a level of maturity to qualify them for their role, but this shouldn't become a system where 'health' is then assumed from that point forward.

Leaders are real people. The leaders in your life—your pastor, your parents, your boss, the teacher you listen to on the radio as you drive to work—are still flawed human beings, no matter how professional their image might be. We must give these leaders permission to be real! We should encourage them to pursue personal spiritual health and growth at every turn.

The need for personal development (not leadership skill development) is even greater *after* someone becomes a leader than it was *before* they were given the office. Yet, almost all personal development opportunities for leaders exist on the preparation journey for leadership. We need to flip the script, turn this around, and make ongoing personal health a priority for all leaders.

Make Necessary Adjustments.

Christian leaders don't plan to have their ministry end in some kind of moral failure, but perhaps they don't implement enough healthy standards and guardrails to prevent it! Before we concern ourselves with what others should be doing in this area, this is a golden opportunity to turn the mirror onto our own lives. You see, the truth is most of us are leaders. We may not like or use the term, but almost everyone I know has leadership somewhere—in a classroom, as a parent, in a church, or on the job. We have people who look up to us for guidance, wisdom, or direction.

If this is the case, then we would do well to use all of these stories of failures as reminders that no one is immune to sin. No one is above heading down a path that leads to destruction, given enough time and isolation from those who could help. So, we should ask ourselves, in light of this pandemic of leadership failure, what do *I* need to adjust in *my* life?

There are a few questions we could ask ourselves as a type of quick self-assessment:

- With whom am I being rigorously honest on a regular basis?
- Who around me has permission to challenge me and even offer a loving rebuke?
- Who do I go to for godly advice and even professional counsel?
- Who knows about my personal commitments to spiritual, physical, emotional, and relational health?

If the answer to any of these questions is, "No one," then this is an area well worth our attention, no matter if we are leading one thousand people, a small group, or only one other person.

Let us take to heart the admonition of the writer of the Epistle to the Hebrews:

"Therefore, since we are surrounded by such a great cloud of witnesses, let us throw off everything that hinders and the sin that so easily entangles. And let us run with perseverance the race

marked out for us, fixing our eyes on Jesus, the pioneer and perfecter of faith. For the joy set before him, he endured the cross, scorning its shame, and sat down at the right hand of the throne of God. Consider him who endured such opposition from sinners, so that you will not grow weary and lose heart" (Hebrews 12:1-3).

Chapter 11

Strength Made Perfect in Weakness

The Book of Judges is a rather dark and gloomy narrative about how God's people simply cannot get it right: stuck in the vicious cycle of "doing evil in the sight of Yahweh," God sending nations to oppress the Israelites, and then God's people crying out to God. This is usually followed by God sending aid, usually in the form of a judge or would-be deliverer. The one thing God's people lacked through the whole ordeal is "undivided allegiance to God. The only thing that could actually bring them peace and stability. Unfortunately, their tendency is to gravitate to human leaders and political structures for security, brushing past God more often than not.

Gideon – Man of Weakness

Gideon is the heart and soul, the pivotal figure of Judges. This man pictures for us a God of salvation and redemption. Surprisingly, when we first meet him, he is a picture of humanity in weakness and fear. But this account of Gideon is a story of growing faith and trust in a living God. In the book of Judges, you will encounter several of the judges whom God raised up to deliver the nation, but Gideon is exceptional because of his weakness.

You see, throughout the Old and New Testaments, God is notorious for using people who are of weaker status, weaker faith, weaker morale, weaker intelligence… weaker everything! Why is that? In 2 Corinthians 12, the apostle Paul pleaded with the Lord to remove the thorn in his flesh; *"But he said to me, "My grace is sufficient for you, for my power is made perfect in weakness." Therefore, I will boast all the more gladly about my weaknesses, so that Christ's power may rest on me"* (2 Corinthians 12:9). The Greek for "made perfect" in this verse is *teleo*, which means to conclude or complete, end, finish, or fulfill. In this context, the Lord is saying His power is *completely fulfilled* in our weakness.

In Judges 6, Israel is oppressed by Midian, so God calls Gideon to bring Israel out of this seven-year oppression. Gideon was a military leader and prophet and, as it turns out later, the greatest judge who reigned. However, what we read throughout his story is that he was very timid and weak in faith. In verses 11 through 24 of chapter 6, The angel of the Lord appears face to face with Gideon to tell him He is sending him to defeat the Midianites. Like Moses before him, he objects by saying his *"clan is the weakest"* and *"I am the least in my father's house."*

Later that night, the LORD gave Gideon instructions on how to destroy the altar of Baal and the Asherah that the Midianites had built. Gideon complies, but because he is so afraid of the men in the town (and weak in faith), he opts to follow God's command in the nighttime instead of daytime, again, despite the LORD saying He is with him. In Judges 6:36–40, Gideon tests God by asking for a sign that He will, in fact, save Israel by his hand. After God gives him a sign once, Gideon asks again for another sign. Not only is he violating the Mosaic law of testing God, but he is still very weak in faith. He saw the Lord face to face, was told the LORD would be with him, spared his life from the men of Midian after he destroyed the false gods, and performed two signs. What more does he need, you might ask?

After this, God tells Gideon to listen to the men of Midian at their camp so he will have more proof that God will hand them over to Israel through him. To bring more comfort to him, the Lord said to him *if he were afraid to go down, he should go down to the camp with Purah, his servant.* Not only did God offer more proof without Gideon asking (because God knows his weak faith), but He also told him to bring someone so he would not melt with fear, which mirrors his fear when he was instructed to destroy the false gods. God is so gracious and patient with his children!

Despite his ridiculous antics and shaking knees, God was extremely gracious to Gideon, giving him all he asked for and more (not to mention the Midianites were defeated by only 300 men to their thousands). God could have very well moved on and chosen someone who would not be so whiny about everything! But God chooses weak vessels in order that his strength may be revealed in them. Gideon reminds us of how we tend to handle things with God. Unfortunately, Gideon is not alone. There are many of us who, seeing the Lord face to face, would still ask for more proof. Sometimes, we try to conform God to our likeness, our desires, needs and wants, and we completely overlook how much He already accommodates *us* in our weak faith.

God promises Gideon that he will be with him. "I will be with you" – a phrase repeated twice in the text is the promise that God makes to him. Gideon imagines that the God of his fathers has deserted them, but, on the contrary, God appears and reasserts his covenant promise to Gideon: "I will not forsake you or leave you, I will be with you." Many of us, I think, can relate to Gideon. I can feel his deep ache of inadequacy, the pain of unworthiness. It is an ache that really isn't based on reality — it is based on feelings, not facts — but it is real, nevertheless. This is probably one of the most difficult problems facing young people today.

The ache of inadequacy and the pain of unworthiness are some of the factors that are preventing many young adults from stepping out and finding their own way in this world. Many stay close to home, afraid of some of the problems that are so prevalent in our world today. We face many social problems — pandemics, sexual abuse, sexual promiscuity, economic hardships, violence, and political upheaval of all types — but I would say that these deep-seated feelings of inadequacy, which are at epidemic proportions, often lie at the root of other social problems – manifestations of anger, depression, jealousy, and strife, often arise out of these deep-seated feelings of inadequacy.

Gideon was a troubled, confused, disenchanted young man, but then he encountered the living God and he built an altar and named it Yahweh Shalom — the Lord is peace. Why do you think he named it that? Certainly, he was concerned about dying after seeing the angel of the Lord — although his fears subsided following God's reassurance. But I think it was more than that. Gideon trusted in the grace and mercy of God. He had admitted his weakness, and yet he was accepted. He had expressed his confusion and had not been hammered. He had expressed his lack of faith and yet had been given an assignment.

There is a great deal of freedom that comes with being honest with oneself and with God. Gideon admitted his weakness, and then he was free and at peace. That was why he built an altar and named it Yahweh Shalom. So we have had our first encounter with Gideon — a weak, failing, insignificant, inadequate, and fearful man. But God called him out of his weakness to a life of faith in him. We are not alone. As weak and inadequate as we might feel, God is with us. He is calling ordinary people, men and women like you and me, and when he calls us into service or into battle, what matters most is who God is, not who we are. He does not call us without providing us with the same resources he promised to Gideon.

I am always very thankful that when God looks at us, He does not see us for what we are but for what we can become as he works in our lives. He is in the business of taking weak, insignificant people and transforming them through his presence in their lives. He begins with us where we are, as we are. He knows our weaknesses, failures, discouragements, doubts, and inadequacies, but he does not say, "You get rid of those, and then I can use you." Rather, he comes to us in our weakness with the promise of his presence that will transform our inadequacy into his strength. From observing the Scripture, it would seem that all of God's great men and women have been 'weak' people who did great things for God because they counted on his being with them; they reckoned that he was faithful.

The account of Gideon especially highlights the fact that Israel was more interested in human deliverers than they were in God, as Israel demands that Gideon and his offspring become kings over Israel; *"The Israelites said to Gideon, "Rule over us—you, your son and your grandson—because you have saved us from the hand of Midian"* (Judges 8:22). Gideon refuses and says that Yahweh alone is to rule over his people, implying that God alone is the rightful king (Judges 8:23). In the Gideon account, God intentionally uses a weak man to fulfill God's own purposes, which showcases that it is God who is undeniably working for his own people. God's people, however, fixate on the tool that God chooses to use—Gideon–and not on God himself.

Alvin Frank, M. Div.

Samson – Man of Strength

Samson, unlike Gideon, as we are discovering, is a bizarre and paradoxical figure, a complex character—perhaps one of the most complex human characters in the whole of Judges. All the judges were seen as being unlikely deliverers who led the Israelite armies into battle against their foreign enemies and delivered the Israelites from oppression. At the same time, what sets Samson apart is his special birth and calling from before he was even born. On the surface, it appears that Samson is a much more likely candidate to be Israel's deliver.

Samson is fearless and bold and displayed none of the hesitancy that some of the other deliverers, namely Gideon, manifested. Although Samson was such a huge force to reckon with in his delivering significant damage to Israel's enemies, in many ways, he is ultimately a failure, and in some ways, provides a kind of mirror image of the Israelites collectively. Throughout his life, Samson blatantly disregards the moral standards set out by God. Samson's clear self-interest is reflective of Israel's own self-interest and tendency to disregard God and God's ways: "Again They did evil in the sight of God" is repeated throughout Judges multiple times.

Though Israel was longing for true rest, Samson's leadership and amazing feats of strength were, in retrospect, the catalyst that got him into trouble. His strength proved inadequate when it came to real deliverance. As we compare the two Judges – Gideon and Samson, we are learning afresh that true strength doesn't come from physical prowess but from God, who endows the weak with strength and causes them to do great exploits. Here's a notable thing. Samson was from the tribe of Dan, which was the weakest of Israel's 12 tribes, yet he was the strongest man of all the 12 tribes. It reminds us again how God chooses his vessels. The tribe of Dan had been scattered by the Philistines, and Samson, along with his parents, was a remnant of the tribe that stayed in the Sorek Valley area, close to the border of the Philistines.

It would seem, then, that this 'weak man' Samson, given his great strength from God, did not know how to use it in a way that glorified God. He had become almost an exhibitionist with his God-anointed strength, 'flexing his muscles' in a self-aggrandizing way in order to gain attention. And in those instances where he destroyed some of his enemies, they were done out of vengeance and rage at those who had wronged him, personally. The following are a few examples where Samson exacted retribution on the Philistines – solely because he himself was hurt and angry (Judges 14-15).

> Samson, enraged that his Philistine wife had betrayed his trust by telling the answer to the riddle, travels to Ashkelon (a distance of roughly thirty miles), where he slays thirty Philistines for their

garments so he could pay his debt, then returns and gives those garments to his thirty groomsmen.

Sometime later, Samson returns to Timnah to visit his wife, unaware that she is now married to one of his former groomsmen. But her father refuses to allow Samson to see her, offering to give Samson a younger sister instead. In an act of revenge, Samson goes out, gathers three hundred foxes, and ties them together in pairs by their tails. He then attaches a burning torch to each pair of foxes' tails and turns them loose in the grain fields and olive groves of the Philistines.

The Philistines learn why Samson burned their crops and burned Samson's wife and father-in-law to death in retribution. In revenge, Samson slaughters many more Philistines, saying, "I have done to them what they did to me. Samson then takes refuge in a cave in the rock of Etam. All of these acts were none, not to fulfill God's call on his life as a deliverer of Israel, but for personal reasons.

The Bible does not describe Samson as a big, burly man; thus, it is quite possible that he was an ordinary man of his day with regard to size and strength. Whatever the case, he derived his strength from the Holy Spirit. His hair was but a symbol of his strength. When he unzipped the visceral and gave up the truth about his strength to Delilah, the Lord left him, and Samson was able to be subdued by the Philistines. The fatal attraction that led him to fall asleep in the lap of Delilah caused him to lose not just his hair but his supernatural power. Because of his habitual sins, the Spirit of the Lord had left him. We read this saying of Samson after his hair had been cut: "*I'll go out as before and shake myself free*. But he did not know that the Lord had left him" (Judges 16:20).

Here are Samson's 10 feats of strength:

1. He tore a lion in half with his bare hands (Judges 14:5–6).

> Samson went down to Timnah together with his father and mother. As they approached the vineyards of Timnah, suddenly a young lion came roaring toward him. The Spirit of the LORD came powerfully upon him so that he tore the lion apart with his bare hands as he might have torn a young goat. But he told neither his father nor his mother what he had done.

2. Samson killed thirty Philistines after his wife revealed his riddle to the Philistines (Judges 14:19).

> Then the Spirit of the LORD came powerfully upon him. He went down to Ashkelon, struck down thirty of their men, stripped them of everything, and gave their clothes to those who had explained the riddle. Burning with anger, he returned to his father's home.

3. After his wife's father gave his wife away, Samson tied three hundred foxes, lit them on fire, and burned up the crops, vineyards, and olive groves of the Philistines (Judges 15:4–6).

> So he went out and caught three hundred foxes and tied them tail to tail in pairs. He then fastened a torch to every pair of tails, lit the torches, and let the foxes loose in the standing grain of the Philistines. He burned up the shocks and standing grain, together with the vineyards and olive groves. When the Philistines asked, "Who did this?" they were told, "Samson, the Timnite's son-in-law, because his wife was given to his companion."

4. For further revenge, Samson killed many more Philistines after they killed his wife and her father (Judges 15:7–8).

> Samson said to them, "Since you've acted like this, I swear that I won't stop until I get my revenge on you." He attacked them viciously and slaughtered many of them. Then he went down and stayed in a cave in the rock of Etam.

5. After the men of Judah turned Samson over to the Philistines, Samson broke from his bonds and killed one thousand Philistines with the jawbone from a donkey (Judges 15:14–15).

6. Samson tore down the gates of the Gazites while they waited to kill him.

But Samson lay there only until the middle of the night. Then he got up and took hold of the doors of the city gate, together with the two posts, and tore them loose, bar and all. He lifted them to his shoulders and carried them to the top of the hill that faces Hebron (Judges 16:3).

7. He broke his bonds after Delilah thought she had discovered his weakness.

With men hidden in the room, she called to him, "Samson, the Philistines are upon you!" But he snapped the bowstrings as easily as a piece of string snaps when it comes close to a flame. So, the secret of his strength was not discovered (Judges 16: 9).

8. Samson snapped the new ropes he was bound with, in another attempt by Delilah to deliver him up for silver.

So Delilah took new ropes and tied him with them. Then, with men hidden in the room, she called to him, "Samson, the Philistines are upon you!" But he snapped the ropes off his arms as if they were threads (Judges 16:12).

9. Samson pulled the pin from his loom.

Again, she called to him, "Samson, the Philistines are upon you!" He awoke from his sleep and pulled up the pin and the loom with the fabric (Judges 16: 14).

10. After the Philistines captured him and gouged out his eyes, Samson cried out to the Lord and finally did a selfless thing. He sacrificed himself. He killed around three thousand Philistines when he pushed the pillars of the Philistine temple apart, collapsing it.

> Now, the temple was crowded with men and women; all the rulers of the Philistines were there, and on the roof were about three thousand men and women watching Samson perform. Then Samson prayed to the LORD, "Sovereign LORD, remember me. Please, God, strengthen me just once more, and let me with one blow get revenge on the Philistines for my two eyes." Then Samson reached toward the two central pillars on which the temple stood. Bracing himself against them, his right hand on the one and his left hand on the other, Samson said, "Let me die with the Philistines!" Then he pushed with all his might, and down came the temple on the rulers and all the people in it. Thus, he killed many more when he died than while he lived (16:27-30).

We see that even with his final breath, Samson's self-interest is still uppermost in his mind. One would expect that at this stage, after all that has happened to Samson, he would be of a more penitent heart, realizing that he is failing in the mission to which God had called him. But instead, his prayer focused on himself –

"Sovereign LORD, remember me. Please, God, strengthen me just once more and let me with one blow get revenge on the Philistines for my two eyes" – as noted above.

However, despite all of Samson's weaknesses, he did turn back to God before he died. God, in His sovereignty, used Samson to fulfill His purpose. In reality, Samson's death did much to impede the oppressive actions of the Philistines. Samson's destruction of the temple of Dagon was a major factor in their downfall at Mizpah by Samuel and the children of Israel some 100 years later (1 Samuel 7:7–14).

The account of Samson teaches us the dangers of pride and self-reliance. Samson lost sight of God's purpose. The Israelites tried to control their situation out of fear rather than seek godly wisdom. However, even in the midst of these misguided actions, we see God's unfailing faithfulness. Despite Samson's flaws, God used these circumstances to accomplish His divine plan. Despite the Israelites' fear, God gave them grace. He can be trusted to work through any situation, no matter how imperfect we are or how challenging our circumstances. Samson's story is a reminder to us to surrender our own plans, seek God's wisdom, and place our trust in Him.

There are many valuable lessons to be gleaned from the story of Samson and Delilah. Though born with unbelievable potential,

Samson forfeits his life because of sin. The lesson for us is that the deeper we allow ourselves to be influenced by the glamour and allurement of sin, the more blind we become. This extraordinary story tells us that Samson was spiritually blind long before his eyes were gouged out. We must accept the reality that sin can seep deep into in our lives. We must know that sin has a blinding, desensitizing impact upon us. Otherwise, we find ourselves ensnared by it, just as Samson did.

We can learn from this account of Samson that God can use the wicked as well as the righteous to accomplish His will. We also discover that our own righteousness or wickedness will not deter God from doing His will. Though God punishes wrongdoing, He may wait to deliver the punishment. Samson also demonstrates that he was a shallow, vengeful man who pouted when things didn't go his way. This, too, was the same mindset of the Philistines). It's strikingly akin to the world's mindset today and contrary to the teachings of Jesus.

All sin, especially sexual sin, comes with its own dire and sometimes deadly consequences. Sin blinds us, then it binds us, then it slowly and inexorably grinds away at us. In truth, sin will take us farther than we may intend to go. It will hold us longer than we may intend to stay. Furthermore, sin will cost us more than we intend to pay. We must heed the stern warning: *"Above all else, guard your heart, for everything you do flows from it"* (Proverbs 4:23).

Perhaps the greatest lesson we learn is that God would rather forgive than judge. In the final analysis, God saw Samson as a man of faith. This is evidenced by the fact that he's listed among those in the hall of faith (Hebrews 11:32). When we read through the list of names recorded there, we find that no one in the "hall of faith" was perfect. Samson was the strongest man to ever live, but it was God who gave him the strength. More importantly, Samson was only effective when he allowed himself to be used by God. In fact, God could have used him without making him the strongest man. He's willing to meet us right where we are right now and to take us where He wants, if we will let Him.

Chapter 12
Guard Your Heart

A Pure Heart

One day, the Pharisees and some of the teachers of the law gathered around Jesus and saw some of His disciples eating food with unwashed hands. So they asked Jesus, *"Why don't your disciples live according to the tradition of the elders instead of eating their food with defiled hands?"* (Mark 7:5).

Jesus replied:

> What comes out of a person is what defiles them. For it is from within, out of a person's heart, that evil thoughts come—sexual immorality, theft, murder, adultery, greed, malice, deceit, lewdness, envy, slander, arrogance, and folly. All these evils come from inside and defile a person. (Mark 7:20–23)

During His Sermon on the Mount, Jesus said, *"Blessed are the pure in heart, for they will see God"* (Matthew 5:8).

What did He mean by the "pure in heart"? Jesus is presenting us with the concept of purity. The word "pure" in Greek refers specifically to that which is made clean by going through the fire or being pruned, as in the case of a vine or a tree. The prophet Malachi speaks of Jesus the Messiah as being like a *"refiner's fire."* He says, *"But who can endure the day of his coming? Who can stand when he appears? For he will be like a refiner's fire or a launderer's soap"* (Malachi 3:2).

To be pure in heart means having no hypocrisy, no guile, no hidden motives. It's marked by transparency and a desire to please God in all things. It's more than an *external* purity of behavior. When Jesus speaks of the "pure in heart," He is referring to internal purity. On the mountainside that day, He wanted His audience to know that their hearts needed to be transformed by the power of God.

I don't have to tell you that it's hard to be pure in heart in your own strength! As human beings, it's much easier to give in to greed, jealousy, anger, lust, selfishness, and pride than it is to keep one's thoughts and actions pure. So much in our world today vies for our attention and tries to lure us away from the things of God. But you know what? That's why Jesus came. God forgave us our sins! And He keeps on purifying us until we're like silver that has gone through the refiner's fire.

If you're a child of God, your heart has been made pure by God. Your responsibility, then is to have such a close and intimate relationship with Jesus that your heart is constantly being purified by His presence. The psalmist David asks: *"Who shall ascend the hill of the Lord? And who shall stand in his holy place? He who has clean hands and a pure heart, who does not lift up his soul to what is false, and does not swear deceitfully"* (Psalm 24:3–4 ESV).

The Heart

First of all, let me state the obvious: the heart, which the Bible so often speaks of, is not that vital organ in the body – a muscle that pumps and circulates blood throughout the body. Neither is it concerned with the romantic, philosophical, or literary states. The Bible mentions the heart almost 1,000 times. In the Bible, the heart is considered the seat of life or strength. Hence, it means mind, soul, spirit, or one's entire emotional nature and understanding. In essence, the heart is that spiritual part of us where our emotions and desires dwell, where we connect with God on a spiritual level, and where God connects with us.

Since God has emotions and desires, He, too, can be said to have a "heart." We have a heart because God does. David was a man "after God's own heart" (Acts 13:22). And God blesses His people with leaders who know and follow His heart (1 Samuel 2:35; Jeremiah 3:15). The human heart, in its natural condition, is evil, treacherous and deceitful. Jeremiah 17:9 says, *"The heart is deceitful above all things and beyond cure. Who can understand it?"*

In other words, the 'Fall of Humans' in the Garden of Eden has affected us at the deepest level; our minds, emotions, and desires have been tainted by sin—and we are blind to just how pervasive the problem is.

We may not understand our own hearts, but God does. He "knows the secrets of the heart" (Psalm 44:21). Based on His knowledge of the heart, God can judge righteously: *"I the LORD search the heart and examine the mind, to reward each person according to their conduct, according to what their deeds deserve"* (Jeremiah 17:10). Jesus pointed out the fallen condition of our hearts in Mark 7:21-23: *"For it is from within, out of a person's heart, that evil thoughts come—sexual immorality, theft, murder, adultery, greed, malice, deceit, lewdness, envy, slander, arrogance, and folly. All these evils come from inside and defile a person."* Our biggest problem is not external but internal; all of us have a heart problem.

In order for a person to be transformed into the image of Christ and receive the salvation of God, then the heart must be changed. This only happens by the power of God in response to faith. *"With the heart one believes unto righteousness"* (Romans 10:10). In His grace, God can create a new heart within us (Psalm 51:10; Ezekiel 36:26). He promises to *"revive the heart of the contrite ones"* (Isaiah 57:15). God's work of creating a new heart within us involves testing our hearts and filling it with new ideas, new wisdom, and new desires. The heart is the core of our being, and the Bible sets high importance on keeping our hearts pure: *"Above all else, guard your heart, for everything you do flows from it* (Proverbs 4:23).

Guarding the Heart

Samson was the classic picture of one who has allowed his heart to be left unguarded. *"Place me like a seal over your heart,"* speaks to the exclusivity of a relationship in Song of Solomon 8:6. And although it is written in the context of marriage, the seal here is indicating a metaphor of ownership and personal identification. Samson's heart apparently had never been totally surrendered to the Lord. Through the lusts of the flesh, he became a friend of the world. The life of Samson is a tragic story of the cost of yielding to the lusts of the flesh. His life is recorded in God's Word as a picture of the destructive power of sin.

Samson often lived in the lust of the flesh; he often walked by the lust of the eyes and often responded with the pride of life. The greatest enemy Samson had was himself. He not only left his heart unguarded but left out a 'welcome mat' – an invitation to have his sinful desires fed. This should be a warning, not just to some but to all of us. Because all of us have the same problem—it is called our flesh. Within each of us, a traitorous inclination against God never slumbers and always smolders. Given any amount of fuel either through the desires of the body, the desires of the eyes, or the pride of life—and it blazes to life in a conflagration of destruction.

Among the host of witnesses we see in the book of Hebrews, Samson is remembered as a man of faith. But from an earthly perspective, he is remembered as a man who disqualified himself by living a life of excess, sexual immorality, and presumption about the grace and mercy of God. Hebrews 11:32 cites him for his faith in God's Word, but apart from this, very little can be said on his behalf. So, *"Let him who thinks he stands take heed lest he fall"* (1 Cor. 10:12, NKJV).

How to Guard the Heart?

So how do the followers of Jesus guard their hearts from the devil that prowls and seeks to destroy. When I was in secondary school, my class went out every morning for PT (physical training). During some of these sessions, we would learn the art of boxing. The instructor would always say, "Keep your guard up," meaning always guard the face. Later in college, away from home, such training helped me to protect myself. When I got married and we bought a house, and our first child came along, we babyproofed the house to keep her from harm. You see, we all have an instinct to protect ourselves. We're born with an aversion to pain. We protect the things that we value.

Later, when I sought to go deeper in my faith, I remember at one of our men's prayer meetings, one of my mentors said to me, "It's no different with our hearts." I didn't understand what it meant to "Guard your heart." I was told my heart can be deceitful and lead me astray. Perplexed, I wondered how a heart could lead one astray? After all, wasn't my heart the thing that led me to the Lord in the first place? Proverbs 4:23 says, *"Above all else, guard your heart, for everything you do flows from it."* We are told to guard our hearts, but how do we guard it, and what exactly are we guarding it against?

Solomon wrote this proverb because his heart had led him astray. He was one of the wisest men in history, yet he loved the ladies a little too much. He had 700 wives who were princesses and 300 concubines, and they turned his heart away from the Lord. He married foreign women in addition to Pharaoh's daughter: the Moabites, the Ammonites, Edomites, Sidonians, and Hittite women from the nations that the Lord had warned the Israelites about, *"Do not intermarry with them, and they must not intermarry with you, because they will turn you away from Me to their gods"* (Deuteronomy 7:3). Solomon was deeply attached to these women and he allowed them to turn his heart from God – Not unlike Samson.

As Christians, Solomon gave us one of the most important instructions because he knew how great his sin was. He realized the status of our hearts affects who we are, how we feel, what we do, and how we live. Guarding our hearts from a scriptural perspective means for us to be alert, through the power of Christ within us, to what enters and dwells in our hearts. The word guard in this context literally means "to set a watchman over it" but not just any watchman. He meant to filter our hearts through the Word of God. We must make Jesus the watchman of our hearts and soul. We are commanded to keep ourselves in the Word as Jesus becomes the keeper of our hearts.

When we guard our hearts, we are putting the filter of the word of God over it. It protects us and directs our feet from going to places where there are great temptations of the flesh. It puts a filter over our TV viewing and on movies that have various states of immodesty or by seeking out images in magazines and online that feed these evil desires. When our hearts are left unguarded, we are often unaware that we are drifting slowly under the surface of the water, going deeper and deeper, until at a point of numbness, those strange undercurrents sweep us away.

We often find ourselves in these dreadful places because we gradually become friendly with the world, and it is hard to tell where we are or how we got there. You see, every deed begins in the heart with a thought. This thought leads our hearts to an action, and that action can lead us to sin. In other words, "Sow a thought, reap a deed. Sow a deed, reap a habit. Sow a habit, reap a character. Sow a character, reap a destiny."

Therefore, we must ask ourselves some tough questions like:

Am I emotionally attached to anything that God hates? Do I have affection for something that is utterly opposed to Him? Is the world and all of its rebellion and lusts – things that are hostile towards God— looked upon with interest, for entertainment, or even for pleasure?

Now hear the words of the apostle Paul, whom I believe to have been the most disciplined man of the First Century and who wrote more of the New Testament than anyone else. We learn from him in his Epistle to the Ephesians, particularly Ephesians 5:3; "*But among you there must not be even a hint of sexual immorality, or of any kind of impurity, or of greed, because these are improper for God's holy people.*" We need to take a look at where we have gotten to in our North American Culture! If we are not listening to the words of the Scripture, our lives will be slowly squeezed into the shape that the lust-driven world around us pressures us to become.

Why Do We Guard Our Hearts?

We know we need to guard our hearts, but how are we supposed to do that, and why should we? If we do not guard our hearts, they are exposed to any bad outside influence, thought, or force that comes their way. This force comes from temptations stemming from our human condition and our enemy. The first few chapters of the Bible capture our enemy in his true character. When he deceived Eve, he even quoted Scripture—albeit twisted and distorted. Satan cleverly led Eve and Adam into choosing to sin against God by eating the forbidden fruit from the Tree of Life in the middle of the garden. The fallout from that dark day is found as an overarching theme throughout the Old Testament, as the Bible tells us how the Israelites struggled with sin. Jesus, however, came to rescue us from ourselves and our enemy, the devil, also known as Satan.

When we guard our hearts, we become aware of God's leading. We become aware of our thoughts, actions, and the words that come out of our mouths. We want to be bearers of His light and goodness in a dark world where our enemy prowls at the edges of darkness. We want to shine a light on the path so others can be led to our Savior. And since Satan's favorite weapon to use against us is deceit, the only way to counter him is with the Truth. The Bible is "alive and active." Hebrews tells us, *"For the word of God is alive and active. Sharper than any double-edged sword, it penetrates even to dividing soul and spirit, joints and marrow; it judges the thoughts and attitudes of the heart"* (Hebrews 4:12) Yes, the Truth is the perfect protection against our enemy.

In the Epistle of 1 Peter 5:8-9, Peter tells us, *"Be alert and of sober mind. Your enemy the devil prowls around like a roaring lion looking for someone to devour. Resist him, standing firm in the faith, because you know that the family of believers throughout the world is undergoing the same kind of sufferings."* Satan prowls around like a hungry lion, looking for men and women whom he may deceive and devour. Now, we do need to be careful about overestimating the influence that Satan has. He is not equal to our God and is subject to His sovereign decree (Job 1:1–2:10; Eph. 1:11).

However, he is a powerful enemy who can influence or tempt us, just like he did to Eve and Adam. He's a professional at spinning a web of lies, craftily sowing doubt about the goodness of God, how we're supposed to live, and so on. If we don't guard our hearts, this can lead to a multitude of issues. The biggest root problem being that our hearts can become hardened to the Lord and His leading. Having a hard heart makes it incredibly difficult to obey Christ. This means we fall prey, and we become susceptible to deception (James 1:14–17).

When we guard our hearts, we are empowered to not only read the Word but also be doers of the Word. It empowers us to live lives obedient to Christ. We do this by loving the Lord with all our hearts, mind, and strength. We put Him first in all we do; Work, school, marriage, parenting, and finances. We seek what His will is for our lives, and we do the best we can to be the hands and feet of Christ outside the four walls of our church. We keep our hearts in check to ensure no one, but Christ sits on the throne of our hearts. This includes checking our pride and intentions in all we say and do.

So, what does this mean for us? We must seek the Holy Spirit's help in aligning our lives with the word of God. We cannot try to guard our hearts in our own strength. We have seen the failure of Samson as he tried to do so. He often mistook his strength as something that he could have manufactured at will. He did not acknowledge his own weakness before God but presumed that there would always be supernatural strength when he needed it. As we all now know, he was quite mistaken.

Therefore, we should prayerfully seek the Lord, trusting the One who gave us a new heart to protect it. We do so by making the worship of God a way of life where we take nothing for granted and seek to build those daily 'altars' along the journey and have a thankful heart that responds in praise to God for all that he has done for us.

We should filter all of our decisions, thoughts, circumstances, and responses through God's Word. Colossians 3:16 says; *"Let the message of Christ dwell among you richly as you teach and admonish one another with all wisdom through psalms, hymns, and songs from the Spirit, singing to God with gratitude in your hearts.*" Dwell means "to live in" or "to be at home." We must allow the Word of God to live in us and have a home in our hearts and minds. In so doing, it becomes a 'filter' for not just what we do but also what we think about. And finally, we should actively set the Word of God as a 'watchman' over our soul by being in the word on a daily basis.

Guard Against A Hardened Heart

We should be careful to always let our hearts remain soft and malleable in the hands of the Lord. Have you built a wall around your heart to protect yourself from getting hurt? While this may help to guard your heart, it may also be harmful if we allow our hearts to become hard towards others and towards God. We can learn to set healthy boundaries in ways that protect our hearts from hardening and becoming bitter. Personal boundaries are meant to keep us healthy, not punish other people.

God cares about your past hurts and wants you to be able to heal from them. When we allow God to heal our hurt hearts, he softens them and also helps us learn how to guard them in ways that are healthy for us and not destructive toward others. We shouldn't exhibit a vengeful heart as that with which Samson went about God's mission of delivering his people. *"But encourage one another daily, as long as it is called "Today," so that none of you may be hardened by sin's deceitfulness"* (Hebrews 3:13).

Bitterness is one sin that hardens our hearts. Feeling hurt by someone else's actions is not a sin. Trying to restore a relationship by communicating our hurt in a healthy way helps our hearts not to become bitter. But what should you do when someone doesn't care about your feelings or value you as a person? What should you do when conversations meant to reconcile escalate and turn toxic? Part of guarding your heart is learning to find your strength and significance in God alone. We need to be strong enough in the Lord to know our worth in Christ so that when people hurt us, our pain does not derail our day or our purpose on earth. We are God's handiwork, created in Jesus Christ to do good deeds.

Chapter 13
Worship as a Way of Life

When Joseph hears that his father Jacob is dying, he takes his two sons, Ephraim and Manasseh, to his father for a proper farewell (Genesis 48:1-22). Jacob rallies his strength, sits up on the bed, and proceeds to adopt Joseph's two sons as his own, thereby placing them on par with his actual twelve sons. To conclude the adoption ceremony, a ritual of blessing follows (Genesis 48:8-20). Jacob designates Ephraim (the younger) as the more preeminent–so prominent that, in time, the entire northern kingdom becomes known as Ephraim.

Jacob's blessing of Joseph (Genesis 48:15-16) includes the two sons. The language of the blessing gathers themes from the Genesis narrative. Its threefold character reminds us of the Aaronic blessing;

"Tell Aaron and his sons, 'This is how you are to bless the Israelites. Say to them: "The Lord bless you and keep you; the LORD make his face shine on you and be gracious to you; the LORD turn his face toward you and give you peace" (Numbers 6:23-26).

God is the one before whom Abraham and Isaac walked. God is the one who has been Jacob's shepherd all the days of his life, evoking his own experience of divine guidance, protection, and provision for the journey. The story of God's activity on behalf of Jacob's family is now to include the stories of Joseph's sons, who receive the promises given to the chosen family.

The writer of the Epistle to the Hebrews makes note of this very sacred moment. He wrote; *By faith Jacob, when he was dying, blessed each of Joseph's sons, and worshiped as he leaned on the top of his staff* (Hebrews 11:21). Jacob worshiped as he blessed the two boys, leaning on the top of his staff. Not only is Jacob now an old man, but he needs the support of his staff to keep him upright. You see, he walks with a limp. Can you see him? One hand supports himself on his staff, while the other is raised in worship to the God who has been faithful to him all his life.

As he worships, he might be reflecting on his life – When twin sons were born to Isaac and Rebecca, they named the first one Esau and the second Jacob (Genesis 25). The name Jacob means schemer or 'heel grabber' – one who circumvents in order to gain the upper hand. You see, Jacob entered the world, grabbing onto the heel of his brother. And so, he was named Jacob or 'Heel-grabber'. He lived a life of scheming– acquiring his brother's birthright through deception. He deceived his father, pretending to be his brother Esau, in order to receive the blessing from his father Isaac.

As a result, he had to leave home, traveling hundreds of miles to his uncle's place in order to get away from his brother Esau, who wanted to kill him. As Jacob worshiped God that day, he might have been reflecting on his scheming and how he used trickery to acquire the greater part of his uncle's livestock. This made his uncle Laban very furious at him, and so he set out for home, being pursued by his uncle. On the way back home, he receives news that his brother is on the way with 400 men to confront him. Not a pretty picture. You could say He is between a rock and a hard place.

Now, for the first time, Jacob seeks the Lord in prayer. He prays to the LORD, humbly acknowledging his unworthiness, and for the Lord to save him from the hand of his brother Esau, who was on the way to kill him.

> Then Jacob prayed, "O God of my father Abraham, God of my father Isaac, LORD, you who said to me, 'Go back to your country and your relatives, and I will make you prosper,' I am unworthy of all the kindness and faithfulness you have shown your servant. I had only my staff when I crossed this Jordan, but now I have become two camps. Save me, I pray, from the hand of my brother Esau, for I am afraid he will come and attack me, and also the mothers with their children (Gen. 32:9-11).

Later that night, the *Angel of the Lord* wrestled with him until daybreak.

Jacob is desperate and would not let go unless he receives a blessing from the Lord. The angel of the Lord asked him, "*What is your name?*" Surely, God knew what his name was. But I believe God wanted to hear it from Jacob himself, as a kind of confession of the person that he was – a schemer. So, he answered, "My name is Jacob."

> So Jacob was left alone, and a man wrestled with him till daybreak. When the man saw that he could not overpower him, he touched the socket of Jacob's hip so that his hip was wrenched as he wrestled with the man. Then the man said, "Let me go, for it is daybreak." But Jacob replied, "I will not let you go unless you bless me." The man asked him, "What is your name?" "Jacob," he answered. Then the man said, "Your name will no longer be Jacob, but Israel because you have struggled with God and with humans and have overcome" (Genesis 32:24-38).

During that encounter with the Angel of the Lord, God did something awesome for Jacob. God changed his name from being a schemer and a scoundrel to a Prince. When Jacob worshipped the Lord that day, as he blessed the sons of Joseph, he didn't do so by singing beautiful and inspiring worship songs; He did so by simply reflecting on the past, his present circumstances, and the future that was ahead for his two grandsons. As he worshiped God, his dislocated hip had become a badge of honour – a reminder of his struggle with God, which ended in triumph. From that encounter with the angel of God, Jacob was left walking with a limp. *The sun rose above him as he passed Peniel, and he was limping because of his hip.* (Genesis 32:31).

Most Christians hear the word "worship" and immediately think of music, which is not necessarily a bad thing. Music is a very common way to worship in church and in our communities. However, worship is more than just the music you hear on Sunday mornings. Worship is something we are called to do as Christians every day in everything we do. It has to become a way of life for us. That said, what is worship, and what are some different ways to do it? In this chapter, we will look at worship. What is worship? Why worship? And how can we make worship a way of life?

What is Worship?

The inner essence of worship is seeking to know God truly and to respond from the heart to that knowledge by ascribing to him glory, honor, and praise. It is valuing God, treasuring God, and enjoying the presence of God. It means to hold God in such high esteem that he is valued above all earthly things. And then letting that deep, restful, and joyful satisfaction that is found in his presence, overflow in our daily lives with not just acts of praise from the lips but also with acts of love in serving others.

What does Worship Mean?

Before worshipping, it is important to understand why we worship and what the heart of worship truly is. So, what does worship mean? To worship is to admire something or someone so deeply that your only response is extravagant love and incredible submission to that thing or person. That is what God desires of us. To know him so well, to love him so dearly and respect him so much, that our only response is to live in honor of him every day in all that we do. Worship is a response to his love and his might.

It is extremely important to point out that worship is not about us. Exalting God is not about what you can get out of it; it is about choosing to praise God and trust him regardless of your circumstances because you know him, and you know that he is sovereign, loving, and by your side. Worship is about praising God and giving to him, not receiving. God has already given us life, his Son on the cross, grace, and the promise of eternal life. When we find ourselves falling into worship for our own gain, we need to come back to the heart of worship and worship from the heart.

How to Worship

Worship is a response of praise to the character of God that can be manifested in many different ways. We can glorify God throughout our entire day. Worship can happen anywhere you are and in whatever you're doing, assuming it is not sinful or against God. When you are in a hearty posture of gratitude and reverence to God, everything you do can be used to praise him. The apostle Paul, in his letter to the Colossians, tells us how;

> And over all, these virtues put on love, which binds them all together in perfect unity. Let the peace of Christ rule in your hearts since, as members of one body, you were called to peace. And be thankful. Let the message of Christ dwell among you richly as you teach and admonish one another with all wisdom through psalms, hymns, and songs from the Spirit, singing to God with gratitude in your hearts. And whatever you do, whether in word or deed, do it all in the name of the Lord Jesus, giving thanks to God the Father through him (Colossians 3:14-17).

In the Old Testament, many of the Patriarchs, on their journey to do God's bidding, usually build altars at various points along the way. Doing this is a recognition that God is with them, and it's a way to worship him. After Jacob arrived in Bethel after making peace with his brother, he said to his household and to all who were with him that they must get rid of the foreign gods they had with them, purify themselves and change their clothes. *Then come, let us go up to Bethel, where I will build an altar to God* (Genesis 35:3).

> So Jacob and everyone with him arrived in Luz (that is, Bethel) in the land of Canaan. There, Jacob built an altar, and he called that place El-bethel because it was there that God had revealed Himself to Jacob as he fled from his brother (Genesis 35:6-7).

As we continue to look at the life of Samson, something is glaringly absent. There were no times of devotion, no reflection on God's goodness, or times of worship. There were no times of prayer until that which we find in those last few moments of his life. His journey to deliver the people of Israel from the clutches of the Philistines was never punctuated with times at the altar. Is it any wonder that he seemed to have become so spiritually desensitized that he did not realize the Holy Spirit had departed from his life? A daily closeness and acknowledgment of the Lord is so very important, especially when we are up against the evils of this world.

Alvin Frank, M. Div.

The word "altar" in Scripture means a place of slaughter and sacrifice, where blood was shed and death took place; it symbolizes acknowledgment and appreciation of God, in other words, the "altar" means worship. The word first occurs in Genesis 8.20-22, where Noah sacrificed "clean" animals as burnt offerings to express his worship, and a "sweet savour" arose to God. Altars had to be unpretentious and unembellished with human workmanship but marked by utter simplicity to facilitate and encourage men and women to seek God.

No doubt, altars were used from the days of Abel, who first brought an offering by divine instruction. The later altars for the Tabernacle and temple had to be constructed strictly according to divine design. They all foreshadowed the person and sacrificial work of Christ. The altar teaches us, in type, the importance of daily communion with God on the basis of the precious blood of Christ. It is a place where we go daily to offer ourselves as a living sacrifice as we are instructed in Romans 12:

> Therefore, I urge you, brothers and sisters, in view of God's mercy, to offer your bodies as a living sacrifice, holy and pleasing to God—this is your true and proper worship. Do not conform to the pattern of this world, but be transformed by the renewing of your mind. Then you will be able to test and approve

what God's will is—his good, pleasing, and perfect will (Romans 12:1-2).

Some altars, like those of the patriarchs Abraham, Isaac, and Jacob, were to show that they were in communion with God and that they relied upon Him for care and protection. One cannot help but think how different the life of Samson might have been and how different the deliverance that he wrought for the Israelites would have turned out if he were in the habit of presenting himself daily to the Lord at the altar. The following are some altars that had been built to recognize the presence of God and to worship him along the way:

Moses' Altar Beneath Sinai

It was a very solemn moment in Israel's history when, after hearing "all the words of the Lord, and all the judgments," all the people answered with one voice that they would obey the word of the Lord. *When Moses went and told the people all the LORD's words and laws, they responded with one voice, "Everything the LORD has said we will do"* (Exodus. 24:3). They had committed themselves to keep the whole law, not realizing their utter inability to do so. Having written all the words of the Lord, Moses built an altar under the hill and twelve pillars, according to the twelve tribes of Israel. On this altar, the young men sent by Moses offered burnt offerings and sacrificed peace offerings of oxen unto the Lord.

Some Altars of Scripture

In looking over the Scriptures, we can see that many of the altars mentioned were built for sacrifice, such as the altar of Noah and the altars of burnt offering in the Tabernacle and the temple. The following four altars mark the unforgettable peaks of Abraham's spiritual experiences in the pathway of faith. As we think of the altars that we do build or neglect to build, we can identify with the experiences Abraham had and learn valuable lessons as we travel along the not-so-smooth journey of faith.

An Altar of Praise

This altar speaks of Abraham's call and the scope of the divine blessing that was given to him by the Lord (Genesis 17:5). Abraham is not only the *subject* of blessing but the *medium* of blessing to "all families of the earth" (Genesis 17:2-3) – one of the most important milestones in human history. Without conditions, this covenant has been ratified and will be completely fulfilled. As Abraham arrived in the Land of Promise, at "Shechem," which suggests vitality and vision, this assurance was just what Abraham needed. Having left country, kindred, and family for an unknown land, he immediately faces the problem of the Canaanites in the land – a cruel, corrupt, and callous people. Abraham and his company would be very vulnerable in this hostile environment.

However, the Lord was with Abraham in the land, and a divine vision and voice welcomed him there: "And the Lord

(Jehovah, the Eternal) appeared unto Abraham, and said; *"I will establish my covenant as an everlasting covenant between me and you and your descendants after you for the generations to come, to be your God and the God of your descendants after you"* (Genesis 17:7). Thus, all his fears were allayed. The promise was renewed, and Abraham was reassured. Abraham had already been unconditionally blessed, but now God reassured him that his seed would possess the land. How does Abram respond to the grace of God? He lifted his voice in praise, and there he built an altar unto the Lord, who appeared unto him.

An Altar of Prayer

As Abraham progressed on his journey, he moved from the lowlands (the plain) to a mountain – the higher ground of faith, so to speak. May this be our desire: "Lord, plant my feet on higher ground." Here, faith found a new perspective; Abraham pitched his tent between Bethel (House of God) and Ai (heap of ruins), signifying duty to God and duty to the world – worship, and witness. *"From there he went on toward the hills of Bethel and pitched his tent, with Bethel on the west and Ai on the east. There he built an altar to the Lord and called on the name of the Lord"* (Genesis 12:8). The "tent" and the "altar" now characterized Abram, and he became a pilgrim, moving from place to place, settling nowhere, *"For he was looking forward to the city with foundations, whose architect and builder is God"* (Hebrews 11:10).

An Altar of Peace

When Abraham and Lot had acquired flocks and herds; strife and division broke out among the herdsmen so that they could no longer dwell together. Abram pleads with Lot not to allow any strife between them. Abraham nobly allowed Lot first choice of the land, and what a fateful choice it proved to be, as he chose the well watered plains toward Sodom and Gomorrah. The yieldingness and generosity of Abraham diffused the situation, and he was rewarded by being given further divine assurances that all the land within his vision would be for him and his innumerable seed. Thus, Abraham moved to Mamre in Hebron. He was now separated from Egypt, free from strife, and enjoying complete security; hence he built there an altar unto the Lord to enjoy the peace and presence of God. *So Abram went to live near the great trees of Mamre at Hebron, where he pitched his tents. There, he built an altar to the LORD* (Genesis 13:18).

An Altar of Provision

This fourth altar is the most important of all – it was for Abraham, and it is for us. Note the emotional pressure. As Abraham was building this altar on Mount Moriah, his heart must have been breaking, for he was about to offer up to God his only beloved son, not only to be slain but to be burnt to ashes as a burnt offering. He knew God must have Isaac, even though he was the heir of promise, so he raised the sacrificial knife, believing that God was able to raise him up, even from the dead. (Heb 11:19). But what was thought to be a moment of death became a moment of triumph – a substitute, a provision, was found, and Isaac was spared.

The substitute was the glorious type of Calvary, where God did not spare his own son but delivered him up for us all. It has rightly been said that "God did not want Isaac, He wanted the heart of Abraham; Abraham was really upon the altar, not Isaac! This supreme trial marked the summit of Abraham's faith. It had been a long and eventful journey of faith from Ur to Moriah, from idolatry to worship, in spirit and in truth. Are you on the altar for God, have you experienced your Moriah? Paul appeals, *"Therefore, I urge you, brothers and sisters, to offer your bodies as a living sacrifice, holy and pleasing to God – this is your true and proper worship"* (Romans 12.1).

David's Altar

When David sent Joab to number the children of Israel, even the captain of the host knew that David was doing wrong and sought to dissuade him from his purpose. Joab was not a man who lived near the Lord, but he was naturally shrewd, and David should have realized that when such a man as Joab knew that his course was wrong, it must have been wrong. Each time Israel was numbered, each man was to give a ransom of half a shekel of silver, but it would seem that the ransom money was not paid. (The people may not have had the money to pay or may not have been willing to do so.)

When faced with the choice of famine, fleeing before his enemies, or pestilence, David chose to fall into the hands of the Lord, knowing that "His mercies are great". But the judgment had to fall upon Israel to vindicate the word of God; *"When the angel stretched out his hand to destroy Jerusalem, the LORD relented concerning the disaster and said to the angel who was afflicting the people, "Enough! Withdraw your hand."* (2 Samuel 24:16). The destroying angel was by the threshing place of Araunah the Jebusite when his hand has stayed, and Gad the prophet came to David, and said unto him, "Go up and build an altar to the Lord in the threshing floor of Araunah" (2 Samuel 24:18).

Elijah's Altar

When Elijah gathered Israel to Mount Carmel, he built his altar of twelve stones, according to the number of the tribes of the sons of Jacob – the altar of the Lord that had been broken down (1 Kings 18:30-31). His mission was to recover Israel for the Lord, Jehovah. He began by gathering the people and repairing the altar, recognizing that there were twelve tribes, even if the kingdom was divided at that time. God answered the faith of His servant, for the burnt offering, which was on the altar that he built, was consumed by fire from heaven. The fire consumed the wood, the stones, the dust, and the water that had been abundantly poured on the burnt offering. This wonderful intervention of God caused the people to fall on their faces and cry out in worship of God.

We Have an Altar

As Christians, we, too, have an altar. In looking at the two systems – Christianity with Judaism, the writer of the Epistle to the Hebrews often contrasts them, and in chapter 13, writes, *"We have an altar from which those who minister at the tabernacle have no right to eat"* (Heb. 13:10). As Christians, we have communion with God through the death of Christ, a communion which Judaism does not have. Our place before God is in the redemption secured by the precious blood of Christ, foreshadowed in the blood taken into the holiest on the day of atonement. *"Therefore, since we have a great high priest who has ascended into heaven, Jesus the Son of God, let us hold firmly to the faith we profess"* (Hebrews 4:14).

So, although the altar that we do have is not one that is made of wood, stones, or any other physical material, it is as essential and effective as those built by the Patriarchs of old. Our altar is our heart, the place where the Holy Spirit dwells in us. Just like the Israelite's altar, our heart is where the right relationship with God begins. When we consider all the hard work, time, energy, and discipline it took the Israelites to maintain their relationship with God, it should be a humbling thought for us.

How often do we prioritize the "important" tasks in our lives over our relationship with God? We should not relegate spending time in God's word only to those periods when we have extra time at the end of the day or as a quick notification by an app every morning. We must prioritize our worship in such a way that the best of our time, energy, finances, talents, and gifts are used to build God's kingdom instead of ours.

Friend, the most important thing we can do is take care of our hearts, protect our altar, and keep it holy. We need to prioritize the condition of our hearts over everything else. Build your altar first. When you do, you will find that God's plan for you is worth the sacrifice. A child of God can raise an altar of prayer, praise, worship, thanksgiving, and sacrificial giving unto God. The state of our altar reflects the state of our worship and our relationship to God.

It is great to respond to altar calls during services in the church. But it is equally crucial, and probably even more so, to ensure that we respond to the private altar calls that the Holy Spirit makes to us privately from time to time. Whenever we sense a distinct presence of the Lord; whenever we receive favor that is unquestionably divine; whenever we know without a shadow of a doubt that God has protected, provided, or intervened on our behalf, we must pause and "build an altar" and worship.

Worship as a Way of Life

Have you ever found yourself leaving a Sunday worship service saying to yourself, "The worship was great—I can't wait for next week?" Or maybe you've had the opposite reaction: "I love this church, but the worship was not my favorite." No matter which situation you have found yourself in, we can all admit that we sometimes equate worship with the music we sing on a Sunday morning. Our perspective of worship is often limited to what we experience at church. But Scripture is clear about what worship is— it extends much deeper than the songs that we sing. Worship is an intimate expression of gratitude for the mercies of God that he's given to his people. And singing is just one aspect of how we worship. True worship happens when we live a life of sacrifice— when we worship as a lifestyle.

Worshiping in Spirit and truth means we are led by the Spirit and grounded in the truth of Scripture. We need the Spirit—he moves in us, teaching us to worship, maturing us, and rooting us in truth. Sacrificial worship begins with our relationship with the Spirit. But how, exactly, does he help us to worship? In his epistle to the Romans, Paul says, *"Do not conform to the pattern of this world but be transformed by the renewing of your mind. Then you will be able to test and approve what God's will is—his good, pleasing and perfect will"* (Romans 12:2)

So, how do we worship as a lifestyle? We live a life of sacrifice. We devote every day to God. We worship in Spirit and in truth in a manner that is holy and pleasing to God. The music we sing moves us and allows us to express praise in a unique and creative way. But music isn't the main avenue of worship—our lives are the ultimate vehicle of worship to our savior. How do you worship? How are you devoting your life in surrender to God? " *Through Jesus, therefore, let us continually offer to God a sacrifice of praise—the fruit of lips that openly profess his name"* (Hebrews 13:5).

Chapter 14
Blinded and Bound

It's been a long journey, both in distance and time, since Manoah and his wife had been given the good news that her barrenness was over and that she would conceive a son. It was during a time in Israel's history when the people of Israel were back at it again, doing what was evil in GOD's sight. Therefore, God put them under the domination of the Philistines for forty years. So it was indeed a happy day when the angel of the Lord appeared to Manoah's wife with the good news that she was going to become pregnant and bear a son. The boy would be God's Nazirite from the moment of his birth and be the one who would launch their deliverance from Philistine oppression.

After the usual time had transpired, Manoah's wife (who is nameless throughout the whole story) gave birth to a boy and named him Samson. He grew and the LORD blessed him, and the Spirit of the LORD began to stir him while he lived in Mahaneh Dan, between Zorah and Eshtaol. But one day, as a young man, he took a wrong turn – a turn that began a cycle of downward movements, not just physically but morally and spiritually as well. He saw a young Philistine woman when he went down to Timnah. He lusted after her and asked his father to get her for him to be his wife.

That fateful step on that day in Timnah began a pattern of womanizing that had brought him to this point, asleep in the lap of Delilah, an enemy of God's people. When he had asked for the hand of the young Philistine woman in marriage, Samson's parents, fully aware of God's prohibition against Israelites marrying into the pagan nation, tried to dissuade their young son from making such a dreadful error. His father and mother replied, *"Isn't there an acceptable woman among your relatives or among all our people? Must you go to the uncircumcised Philistines to get a wife?"* (Judges 14:3). But it was to no avail. Samson persuaded them to get her because she was right for him.

This prohibition that God had given was not a racist one or based somehow on the superiority of the races. It was purely based on the foreknowledge of God that if the children of Israel were to inter marry with those neighboring nations, those nations would lead them into idolatry and immoral behavior. God's words always stand the test of time. Now, here is Samson in love with Delilah, one of their enemies. Judges 16:4-5 tells us; *Some time later, he fell in love with a woman in the Valley of Sorek whose name was Delilah. The rulers of the Philistines went to her and said, "See if you can lure him into showing you the secret of his great strength and how we can overpower him so we may tie him up and subdue him. Each one of us will give you eleven hundred shekels of silver"* (Judges 16:4-5).

Samson has disobeyed God, played with fire, and now he is about to get 'burnt.' Delilah with the awareness that Samson has fallen for her, seizes the opportunity to destroy him and have a great payday as well. She tried on several occasions to wrangle the secret of Samson's strength out of him. But she was deceived on three separate occasions. Finally, Delilah pulled out all the stops in an effort to get the truth out of Samson;

> Then she said to him, "How can you say, 'I love you,' when you won't confide in me? This is the third time you have made a fool of me and haven't told me the secret of your great strength." With such nagging, she prodded him day after day until he was sick to death of it. So he told her everything." No razor has ever been used on my head," he said, "because I have been a Nazirite dedicated to God from my mother's womb. If my head were shaved, my strength would leave me, and I would become as weak as any other man" (Judges 16: 15-17).

Samson revealed the secret of his strength – God had endowed him with extraordinary strength, and being a Nazirite, his hair was a symbol of where his great strength lay. On occasions when the Holy Spirit came upon him, he was able to exhibit tremendous strength. He had trifled with God's Spirit on several occasions, presuming that the Spirit of the Lord would always be with him, regardless of how he lived. But Samson was in for a rude awakening.

When Delilah realized that Samson had finally told her the truth, she sent word to the rulers of the Philistines to come immediately because, this time, it was for keeps. So, the rulers of the Philistines returned with the silver to pay Delilah off. In turn, Delilah put Samson to sleep on her lap, and then she called for someone to shave off his hair. As they did, his strength left him, and they began to subdue him. Sin is like that, you know. Once it gets its ugly tentacles around you, it suffocates and strangles you to death.

This time, when Delilah called out, "Samson, the Philistines are upon you!" Samson awoke from his sleep and must have thought, 'child's play'. He awoke from his sleep and thought, "*I'll go out as before and shake myself free.*" But he did not know that the LORD had left him. What a sad refrain! *He did not know that the Lord had left him*! This was the baby that grew to be a judge who would deliver Israel from its oppressors. Tragically, however, Samson is a lesson in squandering one's spiritual heritage and gifts. After Samson lives a self-centered life of lust and the worship of power and pleasure, the LORD leaves Samson, and he doesn't even know it. Stripped of his power, freedom, dignity, and sight, Samson is a source of entertainment and jokes for the pagan Philistines. But God wasn't quite finished with Samson.

Then the Philistines seized him, gouged out his eyes, and took him down to Gaza. Binding him with bronze shackles, they set him to grinding grain in the prison. But the hair on his head began to grow again after it had been shaved (Judges 16:21-22).

Blinded and Shackled

Tragically, that's the inevitable consequence of sin. It blinds and binds those who have taken its lure and have given themselves over to its power. Sin's labor is severe. It leaves you grinding at Satan's mill, where you become a laughing stock by those who all along had been hoping for the fall and demise of the child of God. But we serve a gracious God, who doesn't always give us what we deserve, but with loving kindness, he comes and rescues us from our prison cell by cutting the bindings that had held us bound.

Sin's Blinding

Just as Samson's foolishness led to him being blinded, our sin blinds us. The apostle Peter tells us what our growth in Christ is to look like:

"For this very reason, make every effort to add to your faith goodness; and to goodness, knowledge; and to knowledge, self-control; and to self-control, perseverance; and to perseverance, godliness; and to godliness, mutual affection; and to mutual affection, love" (2 Peter 5:1-7).

That's the look of a healthy, growing Christ-follower. But what if that's not what we look like? Peter says:

"For if you possess these qualities in increasing measure, they will keep you from being ineffective and unproductive in your knowledge of our Lord Jesus Christ. But whoever does not have them is nearsighted and blind, forgetting that they have been cleansed from their past sins" (2 Peter 1:8-9).

Sin's Binding

Having blinded us, sin binds us. Samson was blinded by having his eyes gouged out. Then, he was bound with bronze shackles. Peter speaks of false teachers who work to lure us away from the freedom of truth into the bondage of sin.

"For they mouth empty, boastful words and, by appealing to the lustful desires of the flesh, they entice people who are just escaping from those who live in error. They promise them freedom, while they themselves are slaves of depravity—for "people are slaves to whatever has mastered them" (2 Peter 2:18-19).

Sin's Grinding

Samson was blinded, bound, and sentenced to a life of endless grinding at the prison mill, endlessly, tediously pushing the millstone in a circle, repeatedly, endlessly walking, yet getting nowhere. That's what sin does to us. Promising deep insight, sin delivers blindness. Promising freedom, sin delivers bondage. And promising the greatest of pleasures, sin delivers a sentence of endless, tedious grinding in the very thing that is killing us. The apostle Peter says:

> If they have escaped the corruption of the world by knowing our Lord and Savior Jesus Christ and are again entangled in it and are overcome, they are worse off at the end than they were at the beginning. It would have been better for them not to have known the way of righteousness than to have known it and then to turn their backs on the sacred command that was passed on to them. Of them, the proverbs are true: "A dog returns to its vomit," and "A sow that is washed returns to her wallowing in the mud" (2 Peter 2:20-22

We look at Samson's profligate life and wonder how it was that the Lord was ever able to use him and bless him. But when we look at Samson in that manner, we forget that God is sovereign, and his grace is poured out to the undeserving all the time. Did Samson *deserve* all the power, strength, and victories? No, and we do not deserve any of the blessings which God routinely gives to us either. In Samson's case, Judges 14:4 gives us a behind-the-scenes look at what God was doing: God was using Samson's rebellion and lust to bring judgment upon the Philistines. Get this: God uses sinful, rebellious people for his purposes, too.

Apparently, Samson took this as a license to sin. But we certainly do not want to take God's favor and compassion on our weakness as a license to sin. If we are trusting that God will use us like he did Samson while we do what we want, we will be severely disciplined. However, we should understand that God's grace and sovereignty are so powerful that His will is going to be accomplished one way or the other.

The rulers of the Philistines, now rejoicing that their enemy – the 'Israelite strong man' – had been finally neutralized, assembled to offer a great sacrifice to their god, Dagon and to have a time of celebration honoring their god, whom they believed had delivered Samson into their hands.

> When the people saw him, they praised their god, saying, "Our god has delivered our enemy into our hands, the one who laid waste our land and multiplied our slain." While they were in high spirits, they shouted, "Bring out Samson to entertain us." So they called Samson out of the prison, and he performed for them (Judges 16:24-25).

The Lord did not ultimately abandon Samson. Samson remembered the LORD, and the LORD remembered him one last time. With his last breath, Samson trusted in God to do a mighty work, and God did so that in his death, he has killed more Philistines than during his life. There is hope, then, in this tragic story. Hope for those who seem like they have long since turned away from the Lord. This is the hope of the Gospel: "Jesus delivers".

The Death of Samson

> Then Samson prayed to the LORD, "Sovereign LORD, remember me. Please, God, strengthen me just once more, and let me with one blow get revenge on the Philistines for my two eyes." Then Samson reached toward the two central pillars on which the temple stood. Bracing himself against them, his right hand on the one and his left hand on the other, Samson said, "Let me die with the Philistines!" Then he pushed with all his might, and down came the temple on the rulers and all the people in it. Thus, he killed many more when he died than while he lived (Judges 16:28-30).

Samson's violent and often sinful exploits bring him to the point of trusting in the un-trustworthy Delilah. Time and again, we see her betray Samson's confidence, yet he does not stop giving her his affection; eventually, he tells her the secret of his hair, and he is caught. It is noteworthy that his power did not lie in his hair; this was not magic. The hair was the symbol of his Nazirite vow and a symbol of his trusting in God, the source of his supernatural strength. Samson had lived his life under a vow that either he did not understand or that he grew so accustomed to that he took it all for granted. He let sin take over his life so that he became powerless, blind and a slave.

The question for Christians today as we seek to apply this passage to our lives is this: have we gradually become so ensnared by the world that we don't even know the Lord has left us? We understand and believe in the doctrine of assurance, which is matched by the doctrine of the perseverance of the saints, but we all know of times in our lives when our hearts have grown cold, we have lost our first love for Christ, and we begin toying with the Delilahs of this age.

Samson kept the sign of his vow, long hair, but lost the relationship with God and, ultimately, the power that God had given him. Perhaps we sometimes trust more in a symbol of our religion than in the Saviour himself and consequently lose the power of the Spirit. We can get so used to our slow backsliding that we do not even notice that the Spirit of God has departed and we are simply following our own path and 'running on empty'. Suddenly, we realize we are trapped, enslaved, blinded, and we wonder what happened. The Valley of Sorek holds great danger for us. Let us stay clear with the help of the Lord.

Lasting Consequences

Samson's story is sad, and Samson's story becomes our story when we reject God's leading and calling on our lives. It is important to realize that though Samson ultimately returned to God prior to his death, having done so, he was still blind, bound, and grinding at the prison mill. Sin has consequences, always, and consequences, once in place, are difficult, if not impossible, to remove. No one sins in a vacuum. God's forgiveness of sin does not equate with the removal of sin's consequences. There are deep physical and emotional scars, not only for us but also for those around us.

Better to avoid our Delilahs than to embrace them and repent afterward!

Chapter 15
Hurts, Habits and Hang-Ups

As we continue to reflect on the life of Samson, paying heed to those areas where he begins to become spiritually desensitized, we cannot help but see a pattern being developed. We begin to see how his hurts, habits and hang-ups figured prominently in his downward slide to destruction. There is a saying, 'hurt people, hurt people'. Samson has experienced a few hurts as a result of his habits, which left him with many hang-ups.

Hurts

We have all experienced hurts from time to time; sometimes it is physical abuse, but sometimes it's verbal. Words can hurt just as sticks and stones. In fact, the apostle James, in chapter 3, warns us about the power of words. So it's not the physical or the verbal that hurts the most; being betrayed can cut so deep that the hurt which it causes can never be reconciled. Have you ever been betrayed, especially by a close friend or colleague or spouse?

In Judges 14, Samson held a wedding feast as he married a Philistine young lady, and thirty men were chosen to be his companions. At the feast, Samson gave them a riddle; *"Let me tell you a riddle,"* Samson said to them. *"If you can give me the answer within the seven days of the feast, I will give you thirty linen garments and thirty sets of clothes. If you can't tell me the answer, you must give me thirty linen garments and thirty sets of clothes"* (Judges 14:12-13). But as it turns out, the riddle was too hard for the groomsmen to figure out. So they prevailed upon Samson's wife to get the answer to the riddle.

Then Samson's wife threw herself on him, sobbing, "You hate me! You don't really love me. You've given my people a riddle, but you haven't told me the answer." "I haven't even explained it to my father or mother," he replied, "so why should I explain it to you?" She cried the whole seven days of the feast. So on the seventh day he finally told her because she continued to press him. She, in turn, explained the riddle to her people (Judges 14:16-17).

But before sunset on the seventh day, the men were able to provide the answer to the riddle. Samson became very incensed and said to them, *"If you had not plowed with my heifer, you would not have solved my riddle"* (Judges 14:18). Samson was so hurt by his wife's betrayal that he went on a rampage in order to fulfill his end of the bet.

Then the Spirit of the LORD came powerfully upon him. He went down to Ashkelon, struck down thirty of their men, stripped them of everything and gave their clothes to those who had explained the riddle. Burning with anger, he returned to his father's home (Judges 14:19).

Angrily, Samson went back to his father's house, and as a result, his wife was given to his best man (Judges 14:20). After some days, Samson decided to visit his wife and claim her back. He brings along a young goat, and his intentions are clear - he wants to "go into his wife in the chamber." He looked for her because he wanted to consummate their wedding. But her father stood in the way and would not allow him because she had been given to his best man. Her father assumed that he was so angry and utterly hated her (Judges 15:1-2).

Samson is obviously angry and declares his intention to "do them harm". This time, I have a right to get even with the Philistines; I will really harm them." Samson said (Judges 15:3). Clearly, this will not be the first time that Samson has acted against the Philistines. In fact, this is something of a family dispute, but Samson's immediate reaction is to go against all the Philistines and intentionally seek to "do them harm". The actions do not seem justified, but ironically, he declares himself "innocent" in regard to his actions.

Samson is smart and knows how to rationalize this anger, and he makes it perfectly acceptable for him to act upon his desires. Samson is still continuing to do what is right in his own eyes. He proceeds to execute his plan (Judges 15:4-5). He took the time to catch 300 foxes, tied them together, set fire to the torches placed between these foxes, and set them loose in the "stacked grain and the standing grain as well as the olive orchards" (Judges 15:5). This was during the wheat harvest. Thus, this was a well-thought-out plan with the intention of dealing maximum damage to the Philistines.

This is not a mild anger or irritation. Samson clearly had the kind of anger that makes one feel hot and clouds one's vision. This kind of anger is not so far-off and difficult for us to relate to if we are honest with ourselves. How many times have we experienced 'hurts' that drove us to do vengeful things – perhaps not of that magnitude. But as Jesus said, anger is akin to murder (Matthew 5:21-22). This is more than just a reaction to a set of circumstances; but has a far deeper root.

What does anger look like in your life today? What do you do in your anger? And when you trace that anger all the way back, what does it show about what you love? Anger often arises when what we love is threatened. Many times in life, this can be positive as we seek to stand up to injustice and evil. But, in this case, and frequently in our lives, Samson's and our anger arises from love of ourselves, as our pride is hurt and threatened or obstacles stand in the way of us fulfilling our desires.

In response, the Philistines sought to find the perpetrator of these actions (Judges 15:6a) and when they found out that it was Samson, they "came up, burned his wife and her father with fire" (Judges 15:6b). It was just as she feared (c.f. Judges 14:15): *"On the fourth day, they said to Samson's wife, "Coax your husband into explaining the riddle for us, or we will burn you and your father's household to death. Did you invite us here to steal our property?"* This is a tragic end, and we see how everyone gets more and more hurt as this story progresses. Being hurt can have dire consequences.

It does not end there. Samson hears about it and says, "Since you've acted like this, I swear that I won't stop until I get my revenge on you." He attacked them viciously and slaughtered many of them. Then he went down and stayed in a cave in the rock of Etam. This is a man who is trying to convince himself that he can control his anger - just one more time to avenge himself, and then he will quit - but that will be easier said than done. Being hurt is never the time to react in anger and take revenge.

But aren't we often like this, too, able to convince ourselves that we are ok and that we have our anger in check? Samson acts against them "with a great blow" and "stayed in the cleft of the rock of Etam" (Judges 15:8). Look at the shadow of a man that he has become, that he has to run away and hide in the cleft of the rock in Etam. Samson is back at square one, without a wife, and he has also caused the death of his wife and her father. All this arose because of his anger resulting from being hurt.

So, what is the proper (biblical) way to deal with our hurts?

1. Bring your hurt to God don't run from him.

When you run from God in seasons of challenge, all you're left with is your own limited ability to cope with what you're walking through. On the other hand, God invites us to draw near to him so that we might experience his peace, healing, and closeness, and this is what Scripture points us towards.

"The LORD is close to the broken-hearted and saves those who are crushed in spirit" (Psalm 34:18). "He heals the broken-hearted and binds up their wounds" (Psalm 147:3).

2. Fill your life with God's Word and God's people.

We should fill our lives with God's Word and surround ourselves with people who speak hope and encouragement into our lives, and then, our experience will be much healthier. Because how we respond to hurt and suffering is critical to how we process what's happening and how healing will take place. We should fill our minds with pure thoughts so that we could experience the peace of God he promises to us in Scripture (Philippians 4:7).

3. Don't be filled with worry, overflow with worship.

Something powerful happens when we actively choose to worship through our hurts and suffering. We aren't denying reality, and we are simply redirecting our posture from one of worry to one of worship. Worship changes our perspective. Worship speaks about where our confidence and hope reside. Worship redirects our thinking. Worship places the results in God's hands.

4. Believe that God will turn your sorrow into great joy.

One of the paradoxes of Christianity is that our Father, God, uses pain for our good. Meaning that our biggest sorrows can result in our greatest joy. When you think about Jesus' greatest sorrow – suffering the shame, punishment, and death for our sins, the result was a great joy – the redemption of humanity and the opportunity for a relationship with the living God.

Habits

Habits are rituals and behaviors that we perform automatically, allowing us to carry out essential activities such as brushing our teeth, taking a shower, getting dressed for work, and following the same routes every day without thinking about them. Our unconscious habits free up resources for our brains to carry out other, more complex tasks like solving problems or deciding what to make for dinner. We all have habits and we activate hundreds every day. These habits can be divided into three groups.

The first group is the habits that we simply don't notice because they have been part of our lives forever—like tying shoelaces or brushing teeth. The second are habits that are good for us and which we work hard on establishing—like exercising, eating well or getting enough sleep, reading the Bible, praying, etc. The final group is the habits that are bad for us—like excess alcohol drinking, swearing, pornography viewing, smoking, overspending, etc. We need to cultivate good habits and get rid of the bad ones, but that may be easier said than done.

Bad habits can be picked up quite easily, and if we are called out for starting a bad habit, we usually say, "Oh. It's nothing. I can end it as soon as I like."

I have a couple of 4.5-kilogram dumbbells that I used to exercise in the morning. When I first pick them up, they feel as light as feathers. I think to myself, 'I can do a thousand curls with these.' But before the number of repetitions started mounting up, I soon discovered what started off as just a tiny weight, which I could lift forever, has now become a great weight, allowing me to do only about fifty repetitions. A bad habit is like that! It starts off not too bad, but before you could realize the effect it has on you, it usually becomes too heavy to break.

As Samson progresses on what should be his journey of fulfilling God's plan of delivering the Israelites from their Philistine oppressors, his actions have become predictable. He has developed a number of habits along the way and responds in ways that he perceives to be the remedy for what he is going through. He has the habit of allowing what his eyes see to determine his actions. He has the habit of allowing anger to dominate his actions, which ends up in wasteful pursuits of women in order to satisfy his lustful desires.

Samson tends to exhibit unhealthy patterns that often start as a perceived "remedy" for some problem - some hurt in his life, which ends up turning into a chronic bad behavior or addiction. These behaviors have become repetitive in his life and are the default scripts he runs to when the going gets tough. They continually lead him into trouble in his life. Some common habits that Samson exhibited were abusive behaviors, bitterness, sexual promiscuity, and wasteful pursuits, to name a few.

As we get a close-up of Samson's life choices, we see that he took the rebellious path. Choice after choice leads Samson from one bad reaction to another - from insisting on a relationship that was not God's will for him to killing bystanders to pay off a lost bet, from walking out on his wife who betrayed him to killing more Philistines after they murdered her. His life spiraled down quickly, all because of the choices he made. His bad habits and attitudes create a circuitous pathway that makes his choices backfire, leaving him rejected and frustrated. And this pattern keeps repeating, over and over, ending in destruction. Like we often do, Samson wants so much for everything to be everyone else's fault. But how does one break out of this cycle of destruction?

As noted, discouragement in life is inevitable. We find this in John 16:33: "*I have told you these things, so that in me you may have peace. In this world you will have trouble. But take heart! I have overcome the world.*" We must lean into Jesus, our peace giver, and choose not to focus on our trials and sorrows. We must seek the Lord and his help in releasing us from those habits that usually lead to destruction. When we don't deal with our habits, they become excuses for dysfunctional behaviors.

Samson should never have been in Philistine territory at all. He was meant to be an agent of rescue, but he became an agent of destruction instead. We fall into the same traps – and destruction becomes perpetuated through our reactions to situations of our own making. The catch here is that we often do not ask how we got to the condition of dysfunction. We're frustrated, and we want to blame everybody else for how we feel. Like Samson, we declare ourselves innocent and justified for any reaction we may allow ourselves. But when we see discouragement and dysfunction, we should ask, "How did I create this?" In our case, we should allow Jesus to break those bad habits and set us free.

Hang-Ups

In our modern vernacular, we could say that Samson had a few "hang-ups." These are roadblocks that had kept him from progressing further in God's plan for his life and the deliverance of God's people. They are often shaped by some warped thinking we may have received due to the circumstances and environments in which we may have been brought up. In Samson's case, there were some unhealthy attitudes he adopted as a means of coping with life's challenges. We see Samson exhibiting some common traits and coping mechanisms with which we are all familiar: anger, arrogance, lack of self-control, bullying, people-pleasing and pride, to name a few.

Samson ignores God's promise throughout his life, pursuing his own selfish and sinful desires. He has allowed his hurts, habits and hang-ups to govern his life. As a consequence, he gloats over the number of men he's killed and holds this up as a show of his strength. While God, like the father in the parable, waits for his prodigal to turn from his self-destructive ways and come home. But when we put aside Samson's passions and homicidal rages, if we can, what we're shown by God is his desire to redeem his chosen people in spite of their efforts to undo his promises.

Samson's life is an example for us that God is faithful, loving, and kind even when we're stuttering and stumbling through the life and tasks he gives us. But even when we fail miserably, as Samson does more than once, and even when we're defeated by our own morally bankrupt, self-destructive decisions, God remains true to his promise. He's merciful even when we're merciless. We can become merciless when we ignore the promptings of the Holy Spirit and drift into a state where we are spiritually desensitized.

Chapter 16
Confession and Repentance

It is noteworthy the steps that led to Samson's sin and tragic end.

To have grown up with Samson must have been quite amazing. His neighborhood pals must have stood in wonder at his immense strength. His enemies must have fled quickly. It was like having a one-man army. As a young man, probably in his teens, we get the first indicator that Samson was not going in the direction the Lord had mapped out for him. Taking a walk on the wild side, he ignored all the prohibitions God had set out for the Israelites. He was in great need of God's grace. He begins to live by his desires and not God's. He begins to serve his own lusts and not God's Word.

What was Samson's Problem?

First, Samson was dominated by lust. That passion led Samson to desire a Philistine woman as a wife, which was strictly forbidden by God's Law. In addition, that passion led him to liaisons with prostitutes, like the one with the woman Delilah, who betrayed him for money. How many times do men say no, no, I'm doing that because I love her? No, love can wait to fulfill a legitimate desire; lust can't. Lust always fulfills legitimate desires in illegitimate ways. Do you want to know the difference between love and lust? Can you wait? If you can't, it is lust. Love always waits.

Second, Samson was driven by pride and revenge. He was more moved by anger at personal affronts to strike out at the Philistines than he was moved by the suffering of the people he was supposed to lead. He was more moved by personal revenge for things done to him or withheld from him. He had become selfish and self-reliant and ceased to trust in God, from whom his strength came.

Third, Samson was defeated by himself. We can hardly imagine what Samson, with his great strength and godly heritage, might have been if only he had daily lived out the formal commitment to God that was expressed in that Nazarite vow. We can only imagine if, like his ancestors, he had built 'altars' along the way to daily give God the praises and worship that are due to him, how differently his life would have turned out. The rest of the story shows the tragic end of the believer who will not let God have his way with his heart.

Many prominent leaders in our time have fallen from grace as Samson did. Some have had great ministries of healing, of music, of evangelism, and have built great empires to themselves, and I guess those are the operative words – to themselves – and not to the glory of God. Many have come forward and confessed their sins when the 'writing was on the wall.' Those who have done so have found a place of forgiveness, both from their community and, more importantly, from God.

On the other hand, others, when their sins were brought to light, denied any wrongdoing until their denial became meaningless, as there was overwhelming evidence to the contrary. Unfortunately, those who are found out that way usually never get back to a place of genuine and heartfelt ministry. This was due in part to the guilt and shame that will always surround them.

Others have not only violated that sacred boundary of trust given to them by the people whom they minister to, but they crossed the line into the area of criminal acts. When these are discovered and dealt with, not only are they ostracized from the community, they may be imprisoned for their action. Being a spiritual leader has some sacred trust attached to the office. But even when one finds themselves in prison, it is not the end. Even when one finds themselves grinding at a mill, one can still call out to God, whose ears are always open to our faintest cry.

Nevertheless, the testimonies of numerous spiritual leaders who have fallen over the years, while different, reveal that the actual moral failure was just a small part of some larger issues that were prevalent in their lives at the time. In other words, there were underlying issues, some subtle, some blatant, that caused a leader to go from a place of trust to a place of experiencing moral failure.

Therefore, one must examine carefully his or her motivation when connecting with someone, either to counsel or to confide in.

Confession

It was in prison that God heard the cry of Samson. Samson had violated God's covenant with him. He had broken his Nazarite vow by living a life of excess and a pursuit of the lust of the flesh. And now, as he is blinded and bound, he remembers the goodness of the Lord.

> Then Samson prayed to the LORD, "Sovereign LORD, remember me. Please, God, strengthen me just once more, and let me with one blow get revenge on the Philistines for my two eyes." Then Samson reached toward the two central pillars on which the temple stood. Bracing himself against them, his right hand on the one and his left hand on the other, Samson said, "Let me die with the Philistines!" Then he pushed with all his might, and down came the temple on the rulers and all the people in it. Thus, he killed many more when he died than while he lived (Judges 16:28-30).

Even in Samson's prayer asking the Sovereign Lord to remember him, his prayer was still a selfish and vengeful one. He was asking that revenge be meted out to the Philistines for the loss of his two eyes. But God, who is merciful and full of grace, who sees beyond our words and even our selfish ambitions, heard the prayer of his servant Samson and granted his desire. This gives us hope that when we confess our sins to God, he hears and answers.

In 1 John 1, the Apostle writes, *"If we claim to be without sin, we deceive ourselves and the truth is not in us. If we confess our sins, he is faithful and just and will forgive us our sins and purify us from all unrighteousness. If we claim we have not sinned, we make him out to be a liar, and his word is not in us"* (1 John 1:8-10).

In Ray Carrol's book *Fallen Pastor*, he shares about one Pastor who had developed a meaningful relationship with Tina before his adulterous relationship was brought to light. In retrospect, as he reflected on what had happened, he said this; "The sin of adultery messes you up like no other sin. You become so connected to that person you feel responsible for them, and it's hard to break that connection. It becomes addictive." [10]

Doesn't that sound like the warning the apostle Paul gives us in 1 Corinthians 6? *"Do you not know that he who unites himself with a prostitute is one with her in body? For it is said, "The two will become one flesh. But he who unites himself with the Lord is one with him in spirit. Flee from sexual immorality"* (1 Corinthians 6:16-18).

In moral failure, there are many losses to be counted

- Samson loses his hair, the symbol of his Nazarite dedication, for that dedication had long since been abandoned. God allowed the outward symbol of it to be taken away from him.

- Samson loses his strength but doesn't even know it until he is overpowered. And when Delilah says, "The Philistines are upon you, Samson!" As he awoke from his sleep, he thought that he would go out as before and shake himself off, but he did not know that the Lord had departed from him.

- Samson loses the presence of the Spirit. He did not know how futile it was for the servant of God to try to serve the Lord when out of God's will. Be not deceived, and God is not mocked. When we operate in our own strength, God will let us fail in our own strength. When we operate without heeding His warnings, He will let us live without heeding his warnings. When we operate without walking in the Spirit? He'll absolutely remove his Holy Spirit from us.

What a picture of sin. First, sin blinds, then sin binds, and finally, sin grinds. Ask any person who has lived a life of alcohol, a life of immorality, a life of drugs – they will tell you no matter how alluring it looks, it grinds—as the writer of Proverbs says, 'It is gravel in the mouth.' And all of this began when Samson despised his blessings and defied his parents.

Samson loses his testimony, for he was the laughingstock of the Philistines. Their fish-god Dagon, not the God of Israel, was given all the glory, and Samson lost his life. Samson was a castaway. He had committed sin unto death, and God had to take him off the scene. His loved ones claimed his body and buried him "between Zorah and Eshtaol"—the very place where he had started his ministry (Judges 13:25). As we think about his death, we see God answered his prayers and allowed him to die a soldier's death.

You might say, we're not Nazarites, and we get our hair cut, and we don't stay away from the fruit of the vine and from being near dead people and all that. We aren't in the Old Testament! What's the message for us? The apostle Paul puts it in context for us. He says in 1 Corinthians 9; *Therefore, I do not run like someone running aimlessly; I do not fight like a boxer beating the air. No, I strike a blow to my body and make it my slave so that after I have preached to others, I myself will not be disqualified for the prize* (1 Corinthians 9:26-27)

Disqualified is *adokimos* in Greek, and it is a very interesting word. It's the word in the ancient world that was used in coin making. People learned early on that you could file off part of that gold coin, and if you filed a little bit off a lot of coins, you could get coins without working. So if you found coins with file marks on them, they would be *adokimos*. People would give them back and say, "I'm not taking that coin, someone has shaved off the edges, cut the corners, and ruined its worth!"

What Paul is saying is, after I've lived my life and poured my life into the mold of God's will, if I cut corners and say I'm serving God so I can also serve my lust a little bit, I can have a little secret. But the truth will be discovered in the end. No, says Paul, I'll not cheat in the holiness department, otherwise, in the judgment, God will say that the one who cuts the corners will be disqualified. That's what Paul does not want to see happening in his own life or in the lives of the followers of Jesus.

As we read these things, however, we should always bear in mind that Samson, despite his failures and weaknesses, was still God's chosen and anointed judge, and as such, he is mentioned in 'the hall of faith' in Hebrews 11. God still used him, and there were certainly times when he exhibited tremendous faith. But as you read the Biblical account as recorded in the book of judges, you do start to wonder 'what might have been' if his weaknesses had not led to compromises with the enemies of Israel.

Although there was much in Samson's relations with the Philistines to deplore, he is nevertheless named among the faithful in Hebrews 11:32, and the Lord's purpose in raising him up was accomplished, for he *began* to deliver Israel out of the hand of the Philistines, smiting them again and again, and slaying more in his death than in his life (Judges 16:30). God not only delivered Israel out of the Philistines' hand, but through David brought them into subjection, for it is written in 1 Chronicles 18:1; *"In the course of time, David defeated the Philistines and subdued them, and he took Gath and its surrounding villages from the control of the Philistines."*

Repentance

Christ is Concerned about our willingness to repent.

There are numerous calls for repentance in the seven letters to the Churches in Asia Minor in the Book of Revelation – repentance from sins such as sexual immorality, lack of faith, and lukewarmness. Jesus said to the church in Ephesus, *"Consider how far you have fallen! Repent and do the things you did at first. If you do not repent, I will come to you and remove your lampstand from its place" (Revelation 2:5).*

To the church in Pergamum, Jesus said, *"Likewise, you also have those who hold to the teaching of the Nicolaitans. Repent therefore! Otherwise, I will soon come to you and will fight against them with the sword of my mouth"* (Revelation 2:15-16).

To the church in Thyatira, Jesus said, *"I have given her time to repent of her immorality, but she is unwilling. So I will cast her on a bed of suffering, and I will make those who commit adultery with her suffer intensely unless they repent of her ways"* (Revelation 2:21-22).

To the church in Sardis, Jesus said, *"Remember, therefore, what you have received and heard; hold it fast, and repent. But if you do not wake up, I will come like a thief, and you will not know at what time I will come to you"* (Revelation 3:3).

To the church in Laodicea, who said they were rich, had acquired wealth and did not need a thing, but who did not realize that they were wretched, pitiful, poor, blind and naked, Jesus said, *"Those whom I love, I rebuke and discipline. So be earnest and repent"* (Revelation 3:19).

We must keep in mind that all these letters were written to the church! The question for us is this: Are we open to being confronted with our sin? Are we willing to change, to allow the Lord to mold, shape and correct us as needed? Are we willing to confess our sins and admit our errors? Our willingness to repent is absolutely essential if we are to be the Lord's people. Jesus wants to know, "Are you willing to repent?"

Guarding Against Becoming Spiritually Desensitized

Today, we live in cultures that lure people into a spiritual stupor that gradually desensitizes them to true spiritual and moral values. Jesus warns that the time would come when, because lawlessness abounds, the love of many in the church would grow cold (Matthew 24:12). He also warns through Paul that in this time, people would be so perverse as to be without even natural affection (2 Timothy 3:3). There is no doubt that we live in those times, and it requires a clear vision and a steadfast conduct to avoid drifting and being sucked into following the worldly crowd. God has given our cultures over to allow the carnal mind to spend itself on continuous sensation-seeking stimulation. The lust of the flesh, the lust of the eyes and the pride of life are virtually running wild.

Without a strong resistance to this almost unrelenting pressure to conform, such stimulation will gradually produce a stupor, apathy, and an unfeeling indifference toward the highest priorities of life, that is, our relationships with God and fellow man. In the 'Introduction' of this book, I talked about the gradual stupefying effect of nitrogen narcosis on the diver who has ventured too deep and for too long – how they can begin to feel so 'at home' in an environment that is foreign to their own – and if they are not careful, they can drift away and be lost. If a person does not defend himself/herself against lawlessness, they will lose their God-given love. A Christian must guard himself/herself strongly against becoming caught up in the stupor-inducing spirit of the times in which we are living.

Steps in the Process for Re-sensitization:

In Luke 13:3, Jesus says, *"I tell you, no! But unless you repent, you too will all perish."* In the Greek, 'repent' means "to change one's mind for the better." It involves turning with contrition, the state of feeling sorry for bad behavior, from sin to God. A lifestyle of repentance will lead to a lifestyle of demonstrating God's power! In fact, in Acts 2:38, on the day of Pentecost, when the people asked how to receive the Holy Spirit, "Peter said to them, "Repent, and let every one of you be baptized in the name of Jesus Christ for the remission of sins; and you shall receive the gift of the Holy Spirit." In order to be sensitive, you have to have the conviction of the Holy Spirit. And in order to receive the Holy Spirit, you must first repent!

Romans 12:2 says, *"Do not conform to the pattern of this world but be transformed by the renewing of your mind. Then you will be able to test and approve what God's will is—his good, pleasing and perfect will."* The word "conform" in the Greek, means "to fashion oneself according to, and to hold possession of the mind." The word "renew" means "a complete renovation, or to cause to grow up." Paul was really saying don't allow this world and its habits to hold possession of your mind, instead, renovate your mind to think on things that will mature you and grow fruit.

It's important to think about the reasons why God hates sin. God wants life to be enjoyable, but every sin comes with a consequence. He hates sin because it hurts His children. When you are exposed to something sinful, be aware and be conscious of the consequences at all times, and then change your thoughts to the things of God. Philippians 4:8 says, *"Finally, brothers and sisters, whatever is true, whatever is noble, whatever is right, whatever is pure, whatever is lovely, whatever is admirable—if anything is excellent or praiseworthy—think about such things."* Reroute your thought process to continually meditate on righteousness.

Realize that God will reward you for every sacrifice you make on earth. When you lay down sin, he showers you with favor, peace, opportunities, and prosperity, just like a proud Father would do for a child he loves. These rewards go so far beyond earthly things. 2 John 1:8 says, *"Watch out that you do not lose what we have worked for, but that you may be rewarded fully!"* The word for reward, in this passage, refers to an hourly wage paid for services rendered. For every decision you make that glorifies God, he will repay you in Heaven.

There is not a single sacrifice you could make on earth that could compare to the greatness of the gifts that God can give. He knows our hearts and desires even better than we know ourselves; these gifts will be immeasurably perfect. Repeat this process daily!

Be alert and conscious so that you will not slip into being desensitized once again.

In psychology, there is a behavioral process called conditioning. In this process, a response becomes more frequent or more predictable in a given environment as a result of reinforcement. Just as you must condition your body to run in a marathon, you must condition your mind to be sensitive to the Holy Spirit at all times. Practice it daily, and make it a habit, and eventually listening to the Spirit will become like muscle memory to you. In no time, facing temptation will become easier because the pleasure of sin is no match of the reward of righteousness!

We Have a Lifeline

From the illustration of the diver in the 'Introduction' of this book, the diver is kept from drifting away by a lifeline held by someone above in a boat. The diver feels the gentle tug of the lifeline and is reminded that this foreign environment, which seems so welcoming and so secure, can lead to death if he or she loses awareness of who they are and what they're about.

As a Christian, you, too, are living in a foreign environment. And if you are not careful, you too can be lulled into a state of euphoria, where this environment dictates the standards by which you ought to live, and where the lure to succumb to the desires of the flesh becomes a threat to your kingdom values. But as a

Christian, you, too, are connected to a lifeline. And this lifeline is the Holy Spirit of God. He constantly reminds you that you are Kingdom people and that you ought to be living kingdom-worthy lives.

So let this be a reminder, as the writer of the Epistle to the Hebrews, and by extension, speak to us today. Let it also be a challenge for us:

> Therefore, since we are surrounded by such a great cloud of witnesses, let us throw off everything that hinders and the sin that so easily entangles. And let us run with perseverance the race marked out for us, fixing our eyes on Jesus, the pioneer and perfecter of faith. For the joy set before him, he endured the cross, scorning its shame, and sat down at the right hand of the throne of God. Consider him who endured such opposition from sinners, so that you will not grow weary and lose heart (Hebrews 12:1-3).

This, then, is the sad ending of the 'strong man' Samson, whose physical strength became his weakness when he gave in to the lust of his flesh rather than being sensitive to the presence of the Holy Spirit. *"They brought him back and buried him between Zorah and Eshtaol in the tomb of Manoah, his father. He had led Israel for twenty years"* (Judges 16:31).

He's finally home. This is where he emerged, a special child dedicated to the Lord, so full of promise. Over the previous 20 years, God's spirit was wrestling with him between these two towns. Here, he finds rest at last. And in his death, finally, for the first time, we see a positive action by his family. Samson might have concluded that he belonged among the bodies of his tormenters, but God wasn't having any of that. We might think we are the most wretched creatures alive, but that is not how our God sees his children. We might be down, but we are never out of His reach and his love. God rewrites Samson's conclusions. He rewrites yours as well.

Chapter 17
Victorious in Death

The Biblical revelation concerning the life of Samson can be quite disappointing, really. Quite negative you might say, and I don't think you might have been told the full story at Sunday school! Some people only like 'positive' messages, and if that is you, it is by no means all bad news. What I find interesting, however, is that when God decides to write about His Judges, He spends more time on Samson than anyone else. It might be just possible that God wants us to learn something so that the errors of Samson are not repeated in our lives and the lives of our descendants.

While it is unrecorded, surely a man like Samson, on whom the Holy Spirit dwelled, would have had times of prayer, prayers of deep and fervent repentance after each episode of wilful and wild living. His conscience seemed to have struck him after he attempted to marry the Philistine girl and also when he burnt up the vineyards. And so again here, he may have had a time of reflection as he tried to justify his behavior when he entered the house of the prostitute in Gaza.

Earlier, at Lehi, when the Philistines came toward him shouting, the Spirit of the LORD came powerfully upon Samson, and the ropes on his arms became like charred flax, and the bindings dropped from his hands. He found a fresh jawbone of a donkey, grabbed it, and struck down a thousand men. After Samson had struck down a thousand men, he became very thirsty.

At this juncture, we see a different Samson. He now recognizes that his own personal struggles with the Philistines are much more than that. He is fighting God's battles as God's servant. He is part of that great antithesis between the seed of the woman and the seed of the serpent. After Samson recognized this distinction, God opened up a spring and refreshed his servant.

Because he was very thirsty, he cried out to the LORD, "You have given your servant this great victory. Must I now die of thirst and fall into the hands of the uncircumcised?" Then God opened up the hollow place in Lehi, and water came out of it. When Samson drank, his strength returned, and he was revived. So the spring was called En Hakkore, and it is still there in Lehi (Judges 15:18-19).

Sampson, Blinded and Mocked

After Samson was subdued by the enemy, the Philistines seized him, gouged out his eyes and took him down to Gaza. They bound him with bronze shackles and sent him to their prison, where he ended up grinding at a mill.

"Now the rulers of the Philistines assembled to offer a great sacrifice to Dagon, their god and to celebrate, saying, "Our god has delivered Samson, our enemy, into our hands" (Judges 16:23)

When the people saw Samson bound and blinded, they gave praise to their god, Dagon, for delivering Sampson into their hands. *"While they were in high spirits, they shouted, "Bring out Samson to entertain us." So they called Samson out of the prison, and he performed for them* (Judges 16:25).

Perhaps here, as Samson reflects (in his deep subconscious, maybe), he remembers how the spies sought to destroy Jericho by entering the city and lodging with a prostitute. The way he chose to destroy the Philistines at the end by bringing down the posts of their temple (Judges 16:16:29,30) has some connection with the way he chose to take up the gates and posts of Gaza. Perhaps he remembers his earlier moral failure before removing the gates in Gaza, and now, in his reflection, he is hoping for a similar victory, one which will take his own life in the process. So he seeks God in repentance, wishing to replicate a similar victory for the Lord.

When they brought Samson out of his prison cell and stood him among the pillars, he saw the opportunity to do something memorable. So Samson said to the servant who held his hand, *"Put me where I can feel the pillars that support the temple, so that I may lean against them"* (Judges 16:26).

Now, the temple was crowded with men and women; all the rulers of the Philistines were there, and on the roof were about three thousand men and women watching Samson perform.

Samson's Prayer

> Then Samson prayed to the LORD, "*Sovereign LORD, remember me. Please, God, strengthen me just once more, and let me with one blow get revenge on the Philistines for my two eyes*." (Judges 16:28)

This is an appeal to be shown God's mercy one last time. Even in this prayer, we see that Samson is still not very focused on his mission. He is still exhibiting some very selfish traits, as he has done before, motivated by vengeance. He focuses on vengeance for the loss of his two eyes. It's a bit of a sloppy prayer. It seems like a mixture of intentions. Samson knew that he was not deserving of God's strength. He also knew it was completely up to the Lord to provide that strength. His request for the Lord to remember him is a legitimate nod to God's promise to deliver Israel through him. However, his request for vengeance seems self-serving. There are a number of better things he could have prayed at this point. Samson's prayer is good, but it's filled with impure motives, much like all of our best works.

But God, who has been patient and merciful toward him, answers his prayers. This is a confession of a man whose eyes have been blinded by the Philistines but, once again, opened by the Spirit. The Philistines are not simply the enemies of Israel; they are the uncircumcised, the unclean, some of the seed of the serpent. Samson now recognizes that he is no different. He sees how greatly he has sinned against God by forsaking his calling.

Samson's Death

At this point, Samson sees that he deserves to die as a rebel. But does he? There are two kinds of death: the death that is "capital punishment" and the death of a soldier, the soldier who throws himself on a grenade in order to save his companions – a martyr. Samson dies the death of a soldier, although he deserves the death of a sinner. In fact, he is more victorious in his death than in his life, we read:

> Then Samson reached toward the two central pillars on which the temple stood. Bracing himself against them, his right hand on the one and his left hand on the other, Samson said, "Let me die with the Philistines!" Then he pushed with all his might, and down came the temple on the rulers and all the people in it. Thus, he killed many more when he died than while he lived (Judges 16:28-30).

In all of their frenzied excitement, they decide to bring out Samson to entertain them. Maybe they were asking him to show more of his amazing strength, which would have simply resulted in more mockery, as Samson was incapable of performing anything special. So they thought. Samson's request to lean against the pillars builds our anticipation. Despite Samson's desire for personal vengeance, it is Yahweh who gets vengeance upon idolatrous people. Dagon, their god, is powerless! The capture and torture of one of the Lord's servants leads to the death of 3,000 Philistines.

Unlike in Judges 15:18, when Samson cried out to the Lord: *"You have given your servant this great victory. Must I now die of thirst and fall into the hands of the uncircumcised?"* Now, Samson is prepared to die as a final act of fulfilling the mission of God – a mission that he had not been very careful to fulfill. Samson, a man who is now morally compromised, cries out to the Lord, and the Lord hears his prayers. God is never beyond your reach! We can, at any time, cry out to him in repentance. God knows our hearts even though you don't know exactly what to say. God can open your eyes through the power of the Gospel, even though you don't have the strength to lift your head. Call upon the name of the Lord for your deliverance, and He will come to your aid and save you.

Samson's final act was to lean his weight against the two middle pillars (one in each hand). He cried out to the Lord, "Let me die with the Philistines." And the Lord granted his request, accomplishing his will to bring a partial judgment upon Israel's oppressors: *"He will take the lead in delivering Israel from the hands of the Philistines"*(Judges 13:5).

When an angel comes to promise Samson's miraculous birth, he says that Samson will "begin to save Israel from the hand of the Philistines" (Judges 13:5). *Begin.* That's a strange way of saying it. Who is going to finish it? Samson, after all, is the last judge in the book. The author is intentionally clueing us in because, for the end of this story, you're going to have to look beyond this book. And for those of us who know the end of the Big Story, it should be obvious: Jesus completes the salvation that Samson could only start.

You can even see this in the story of Samson's birth. It parallels Jesus' birth in some remarkable ways: both were promised miraculously before their birth; both were answers to Israel's bondage; both stories skip straight from birth to adulthood, skipping their childhoods. You can think of Samson's birth story as a premonition of the truer and better Judge who was to come.

But even though the parallels between Jesus' birth and Samson's are striking, there's a glaring difference, too. Samson's birth would have brought joy and honor to a woman who (because she was barren) was in the midst of shame. But the birth of Jesus was the opposite: it *brought* disgrace to Mary and Joseph because it looked like they had a child out of wedlock. The difference is crucial because it shows us how the real Savior would save—not through power and honor, but through shame and disgrace.

Samson in the Valley of Sorek

From the very beginning, Samson's story pointed away from Samson. It pointed to Jesus, the true and better Judge, who would succeed in every place that Samson failed. Like Samson, Jesus' strength would reside not in how he was built but in the indwelling power of the Spirit. But unlike Samson, Jesus would never compromise on God's law. He would keep every facet of it. *Unlike* Samson, who was controlled by his impulses, Jesus would be controlled by God's will. After fasting for 40 days in the wilderness, he could rebuff Satan's attempts to tempt him with bread by saying, "I don't live by bread; I live by God's Word." *Unlike* Samson, who felt entitled and proud, Jesus—who actually *was* entitled to a throne—would take the role of a servant and submit himself to the humiliation of the cross.

We may stand in awe of the strength of Samson. But I stand *amazed* at the presence of Jesus the Nazarene. You see, admiring Samson for his strength might impress us, but it can never truly lead us to change. Because what we most need isn't a strong role model, what we need is a weak and broken Savior, someone who would give us his strength and save us from ourselves. And that is just what Jesus did when he died on the cross. In his death he was more victorious than in life. Because in his death, he rescued us from the dominion of darkness. This is why it says: "*When he ascended on high, he took many captives and gave gifts to his people*" (Ephesians 4:8).

Alvin Frank, M. Div.

The irony of Samson is that he was strong on the outside but terribly weak on the inside. In that way, he's like so many of us. We need someone to empower our spirits, not to simply inspire our imaginations. And when you see and believe what Jesus did for you—that he who was strong became weak for you; that he who was rich became poor for you; that the righteous became sin for you; that Life himself underwent death *for you* … then, and only then, will you receive the moral strength to live the way Samson couldn't.

The effects of his death typified those of the death of Christ, who, of his own will, laid down his life among transgressors and thus overturned the foundation of Satan's kingdom and provided for the deliverance, not just of his people, but of people everywhere. As great as the sin of Samson was, and as justly as he deserved the judgments he brought upon himself, at last, he found mercy at the hand of the Lord.

It is a reminder to us that every penitent sinner shall obtain mercy as he or she flees for refuge to the Saviour whose blood cleanses from all sin. But this grace of the Saviour that is so readily available to the penitent should not encourage us to indulge in sin. Instead, it should cause us to walk circumspectly, redeeming the times and recognizing that we are living in evil days.

Samson's Burial

Then his brothers and his father's whole family went down to get him. His brothers – the Bible does not elaborate on this, so it is not known here whether these are his blood brothers or just a reference to God's people. As you know, Samson's mother was barren when she encountered the Lord. But as in the case of Hannah, who was barren before the Lord opened her womb and gave her a son – Samuel, the Lord also gave her three more sons and two daughters (1 Samuel (1 Samuel 2:21). So it is possible that the Lord had mercy on Samson's mother and other children as well. The family brought him back and buried him between Zorah and Eshtaol in the tomb of Manoah, his father. He had led Israel for twenty years (16:31).

Samson was buried by his family members, which shows that they respected him and were reconciled with him. They buried him between Zorah and Eshtaol at the tomb of his father, Manoah. By mentioning the site of his burial, the story returns to the opening stage of our story. There, it says that the spirit of God seized Samson between Zorah and Eshtaol.

This victory is unquestionably the Lord's, even if it is only achieved through the suffering of his servant. We marvel at God's use of Samson as a sinful servant who brought a partial and temporary deliverance for a relatively small portion of God's people. It all pales in comparison to our True Judge, Jesus Christ, who brought complete and everlasting deliverance for all who place their faith in him!

- Samson destroyed Dagon's Temple in his death, but Christ defeated every false god in his crucifixion.

- Samson's death was the end of his reign, but Jesus's death established his reign forever (Phil. 2:8-11).

- Both Samson and Jesus willingly gave their lives, but only Jesus had victory over the grave.

Although Samson was the strongest man to ever live, we see many weaknesses in his character. However, God still used him in spite of these weaknesses. There is a trend in the Bible that God usually does not choose the most qualified person for the job. He chose a bunch of fishermen to bring His gospel to the world. The Lord chose Moses, who wasn't eloquent in speech, to talk to King Pharaoh to release Israel. There are many other stories to mention here. In short, if God chooses broken people to show His grace, he can surely choose any one of us. Praise be to the Lord!

The lust of the flesh was Samson's greatest weakness. It led to his death! Of course, we see our own weaknesses on display. Whether your temptation is the same or some other vice, we can *all* learn something from Samson's failure. What makes this account of Samson's life truly remarkable is that his moral compromise is met by the Lord's covenant grace and patience. The Lord deals patiently with Samson and continues to use him to fulfill his covenant purposes. The Lord patiently works through sinful servants to bring deliverance to his chosen people.

The Philistines put Samson on display in their temple, bound and apparently helpless, mocking him and the God of Heaven. But Samson's hair had begun to grow back in time, and with it, his faith in God. His captors did not realize that by chaining Samson to two weight-bearing pillars, they were signaling their own doom. Leaning against the pillars with his renewed strength, he pushed the pillars apart, causing their fall. With the temple's collapse came the demise of many Philistines, as well as his own. The Philistine's victory turned into defeat, while Samson's defeat turned into a final triumph. (Judges 16:22-30).

Is this not a shadow of the cross? For on the cross, Jesus outstretched his arms to topple the twin pillars of sin and death? Although death pulled Jesus into its bosom, his subsequent resurrection brought triumph from apparent defeat. Of course, Jesus' victory was ensured due to his sinless life, while Samson's defeat came as he succumbed to the wiles of the flesh. But have we not all "sinned and fall short of the glory of God?" (Rom. 3:23,24).

Indeed! But the good news is that Jesus paid the penalty for our sins. And when we put our faith in Him, His meritorious life is credited to us; His victory becomes our victory. Even though late in Samson's life, it was none too late, nor is it for any of us. Through the Spirit, God will give us strength to overcome our weaknesses. But one must turn away from the darkness and turn to Christ. If you do, you, too, will prevail.

Theologians usually find some common ground between Samson and Jesus. However, Christ had no sin, so he had no business dying. Putting Christ to death meant that, for the first time, we had a man who died but did not sin. This means death had no legal hold on Him, and thus, He had to re-emerge from it. In His resurrection, we have all been made alive to God.

In conclusion, the real Judge did more heavy lifting than Samson could ever do in a million years. Jesus Christ lifted the sin of the world, and that is no mean task. Samson defeated lions and the Philistines, and Jesus Christ defeated the real enemy, not the Philistines or the Romans or the Jews, but the puppet master behind sin and death, the devil himself. And unlike those Judges whose deaths usually led to Israel going back to their old ways, the real Judge, Jesus Christ, does not die. His kingdom is everlasting, and there shall be no end to His reign!

The writer of the Epistle to the Hebrews sums up for us how Jesus Christ, who shared our humanity, was able to live a righteous and holy life, delivering us from the power of sin and death:

"Since the children have flesh and blood, he too shared in their humanity so that by his death he might break the power of him who holds the power of death—that is, the devil—and free those who all their lives were held in slavery by their fear of death" (Hebrews 2:14-15).

Chapter 18
Help and Hope for Tomorrow

Samson, the Carnal Man

One of the saddest chapters in all of Scripture is the story of Samson. Here was a man with tremendous potential. He had godly parents, supernatural strength, and the Lord's favor. He literally had more gifts and more advantages than anyone else in his era. He was born and called by God to serve as a living picture of divine deliverance—and in that sense, he prefigured Christ. His birth was supernatural; he suffered for the sake of his people. Everything about him was amazing. He is very much a messiah figure—in every way but one: he was not particularly faithful.

Scripture records several disastrous spiritual lapses in his life. He was especially prone to the kind of carnal failure that stems from unbridled lust blended with a lack of personal discipline. He couldn't control his fleshly desires, and he was a strong-willed man. And that is a disastrous combination. The fact is, if we looked only at Samson's personal character and the external evidence of his sanctification (or lack of it), we would almost certainly conclude that Samson was a miserable failure. He is a classic example of wasted opportunity. He is a vivid reminder that mortal men are totally depraved and in desperate need of a savior.

It is inevitable, therefore, that you, like myself, might begin to wonder just why God chose Samson even before he was born? God sanctified him, made him a Nazirite, and set him apart as a deliverer of the Israelites. Through His foreknowledge, God would have seen Samson's acts of disobedience, his lustful heart, his self-reliance, and his vengeful spirit. You might ask; If God knew all of that, why would He spend so much effort on one who, it seems, is doomed to failure?

Samson, God's Choice

But as I ponder the question a little deeper, a thought is beginning to emerge. In many ways, Samson is a picture of Israel and, dare I say, a picture of you and me! Many times, the Bible uses one person or thing to stand for something larger. Samson personifies the entire nation of Israel in his day. The way he treated his status as specially chosen mirrors Israel's status as the chosen race. Perhaps that explains his preference for foreign women. Israelites, in general, were forbidden to marry them.

When Samson demanded that his father Manoah get a Philistine bride for him, Manoah protested but got him the desired bride. Manoah would have been well within his rights to choose a suitable bride for his son and compel him to marry her. We might ask, why didn't he? Perhaps, then, we should take Manoah as a type of divine love in permissive will. Samson's desire for foreign women also mirrored Israel's desire to worship foreign gods.

The Bible says Samson's choice was from God; (*His parents did not know that this was from the LORD, who was seeking an occasion to confront the Philistines; for at that time they were ruling over Israel*) Judges 14:4. But that can only mean Samson began to walk in God's *permissive* will rather than His *intentional* will. Unlike other times, in the Samson era, Israel seemed quite content under the Philistine rule. They didn't even know they needed deliverance from the Philistines. Certainly, Samson's antics made their rule a little less benign. God accepted Samson spiritual weakness and all and used him to advance his (God's) purposes. But Samson would have been even more effective if he had remained faithful to his calling.

Samson, a Mirror of Israel and Us

I mentioned that I see Samson, not just a picture of Israel, but a picture of you and me. What exactly do I mean by that? We were born in sin and shaped in iniquity. So, we were sinners by birth and sinners by choice. When God looked at us, He could have frowned in derision and passed us by. We were like Israel when God found her. Ezekiel 16 describes in very graphic language how God saw Israel metaphorically:

On the day you were born, your cord was not cut, nor were you washed with water to make you clean, nor were you rubbed with salt or wrapped in cloths. No one looked on you with pity or had compassion enough to do any of these things for you. Rather, you were thrown out into the open field, for on the day you were born, you were despised. "Then I passed by and saw you kicking about in your blood, and as you lay there in your blood, I said to you, "Live!" I made you grow like a plant of the field. You grew and developed and entered puberty. Your breasts had formed, and your hair had grown, yet you were stark naked (Ezekiel 16:4-7).

The picture is emerging even clearer, as to whom Israel was when God found her. It is becoming clearer also that when God found us, we were in bad shape. And as a child of Israel, when God chose Samson, he was no better. So why did God choose him when, in His foreknowledge, God saw his failures?

Ezekiel 16 Continues:

"Later, I passed by, and when I looked at you and saw that you were old enough for love, I spread the corner of my garment over you and covered your naked body. I gave you my solemn oath and entered into a covenant with you, declares the Sovereign LORD, and you became mine. I bathed you with water and, washed the blood from you and put ointments on you. I clothed you with an embroidered dress and put sandals of fine leather on you. I dressed you in fine linen and covered you with costly garments" (Ezekiel 16:8-10).

But like an ungrateful child, Israel forsook the Lord and began to live a life of sin and depravity: *"But you trusted in your beauty and used your fame to become a prostitute. You lavished your favors on anyone who passed by and your beauty became his"* (Ezekiel 16:15).

God's Abundant Favor Toward Us

The Apostle Peter also sees all of us as helpless children who need to be washed and made clean. When God looked at us, there was nothing about us that was desirous to Him. But He had mercy and compassion on us and sent His One and only Son to rescue us. What do we have in common with Israel and Samson? We all needed to be rescued by God, who just didn't rescue us but gave us a bright hope for tomorrow:

The Apostle Peter says;

Blessed *be* the God and Father of our Lord Jesus Christ, who according to His abundant mercy has begotten us again to a living hope through the resurrection of Jesus Christ from the dead, to an inheritance incorruptible and undefiled and that does not fade away, reserved in heaven for you, who are kept by the power of God through faith for salvation ready to be revealed in the last time (1 Peter 1:3-5 NKJV).

The Apostle holds out a very bright hope for us promised by the Lord, who provides strength for the Journey. But we have to live with that constant awareness that we are not our own, that we were bought at a price. He writes:

Therefore, with minds that are alert and fully sober, set your hope on the grace to be brought to you when Jesus Christ is revealed at his coming. As obedient children, do not conform to the evil desires you had when you lived in ignorance. But just as he who called you is holy, so be holy in all you do; for it is written: "Be holy, because I am holy (1 Peter 1:13-15).

The Apostle Peter admonishes us to be holy. How is that possible knowing all that we know about ourselves? Quite simply, we belong to God. He has called us — you and me. Chosen us, set us apart for His purposes. We are different now. We are not living for ourselves. We are living for him. We are set apart, holy. The Apostle Paul says: *Therefore, as God's chosen people, holy and dearly loved, clothe yourselves with compassion, kindness, humility, gentleness and patience* (Colossians 3:12).

In other words, as God's chosen people, we are to do this! Live like this! Being holy means, we live differently than the world around us who does not know or honor Him. The Apostle Peter reminds us that we are strangers and foreigners here and that we are no longer our own. He writes;

> Since you call on a Father who judges each person's work impartially, live out your time as foreigners here in reverent fear. For you know that it was not with perishable things such as silver or gold that you were redeemed from the empty way of life handed down to you from your ancestors, but with the precious blood of Christ, a lamb without blemish or defect. He was chosen before the creation of the world but was revealed in these last times for your sake. Through him, you believe in God, who raised him from the dead and glorified him, and so your faith and hope are in God (1 Peter 1: 17-21).

Because our strength, our faith and our hope are in God, there is nothing about us for which we may boast. Wretched and poor, blind and naked, God found us and clothed us with His own righteousness. He gives us strength each day for the journey, and fills us with hope for tomorrow. Therefore, with thankful hearts, we should endeavor to live this new life, not in our own strength, as Samson did. But let us allow the Holy Spirit to constantly renew our hearts so that day by day, we are transformed more and more into the image of our Lord Jesus Christ. The Apostle Peter says:

> For this very reason, make every effort to add to your faith goodness; and to goodness, knowledge; and to knowledge, self-control; and to self-control, perseverance; and to perseverance, godliness; and to godliness, mutual affection; and to mutual affection, love. For if you possess these qualities in increasing measure, they will keep you from being ineffective and unproductive in your knowledge of our Lord Jesus Christ. But whoever does not have them is nearsighted and blind, forgetting that they have been cleansed from their past sins (2 Peter 1:5-9).

This change of behavior begins on the inside with our attitude and mindset. When our inner thought life, our purpose, and our character are changed into the image of Christ, our outward selves and outworking behavior will alter naturally. This process is the Holy Spirit's work of sanctification: *"And we all, who with unveiled faces contemplate the Lord's glory, are being transformed into his image with ever-increasing glory, which comes from the Lord, who is the Spirit"* (2 Corinthians 3:18).

As believers, we ought to be notably different from non-believers and our old selves because of our relationship with God through Jesus Christ. His holy presence in our lives produces in us a loving obedience to God's Word, which ultimately forms God's character in us. If we are set apart for God's use, separated from our old, common way of living, we are following God's command to "be holy."

The Mirror of God

The reason, I believe, God called and consecrated Samson to be a deliverer, even though in His foreknowledge, He saw Samson's failure, is because God wanted to use Samson as a mirror in which Israel would see herself, disobedient and going after the forbidden. And as we look at Samson, we too can see ourselves – flawed, often selfish and of the world. But God still calls us and uses us as soldiers of the cross, co-workers with Christ, delivering people from the bondage of sin.

As Jesus commissions us and fills us with His Holy Spirit, He provides the enablement necessary to succeed. But as we have seen from Samson's life, although he was filled with the Holy Spirit, he went off the rails. So how do we stay on course so that we do not drift away? As we have seen, becoming spiritually desensitized happens very imperceptibly and not with a giant leap. It happens gradually as we allow the lust of the eyes, the lust of the flesh and the pride of life to numb our spiritual receptors.

Stay Connected to the True Vine

Therefore, with the help of the Holy Spirit's, we must abide in the 'True Vine' and in the Word of God, staying alert to the fact that the battle in which we are engaged is not a physical one – not flesh and blood - but a spiritual one. We are battling the forces of evil in the heavenly realm. Consequently, we must put on the full armor of God, as we are admonished to do in Ephesians 6. The devil's schemes can be cleverly disguised, but the weapons that we fight with, are powerful, capable of rooting out and demolishing the strongholds of the evil one.

So let me end with the verses of Scripture with which I began:

"We must pay the most careful attention, therefore, to what we have heard so that we do not drift away. For since the message spoken through angels was binding, and every violation and disobedience received its just punishment, how shall we escape if we ignore so great a salvation? This salvation, which was first announced by the Lord, was confirmed to us by those who heard him. God also testified to it by signs, wonders and various miracles, and by gifts of the Holy Spirit distributed according to his will" (Hebrews 2:1-4).

'May the LORD bless you and protect you. May the LORD smile on you and be gracious to you. May the LORD show you his favor and give you his peace' (Numbers 6:24-26 NLT)

Notes

1. Sinclair Lewis, *Elmer Gantry* (New York: Harcourt, Brace, 1927), 5.

2. Terry C. Muck. *Sins of the Body* (Carol Steam, Illinois: Word Publishing, 1989), 17.

3. Archibald D. Hart, *The Sexual Man*: Masculinity Without Guilt (Dallas: Word, 1994), 85.

4. Ed Wheat, MD and Gaye Wheat. *Intended for Pleasure* (Old Tappan, New Jersey: Fleming H. Revell Company, 1977), 131.

5.https://www.charlotteobserver.com/article189940794.html#storylink=cpy

6. https://people.com/crime/249jessica-hahn-jim-bakker-tammy-faye-scandal-made-me-famous/

7. Terry C. Muck. *Sins of the Body* (Carol Steam, Illinois: Word Publishing, 1989), 109.

8. Scott Hubbard. Article: *Good Leaders Fail Well* (DesiringGod.org)

9. Scott Hubbard. Article: *Good Leaders Fail Well* (DesiringGod.org)

Alvin Frank, M. Div.

10. Ray Carrol, *Fallen Angel: Finding Restoration in a Broken World* (Folsom, CA: Civitas Press, 2011), 110.

amcontent.com/pod-product-compliance
Source LLC
burg PA
0914120626
B00001B/264